Forming a Community of Prayer

Forming a Community of Prayer

Adrienne Holmes

Warner Press

Anderson, Indiana

Coordinator of Publishing & Creative Services
Church of God Ministries, Inc.
PO Box 2420
Anderson, IN 46018-2420
800-848-2464
www.chog.org

To purchase additional copies of this book, to inquire about distribution, and for all other sales-related matters, please contact:

Warner Press, Inc.
PO Box 2499
Anderson, IN 46018-2499
800-741-7721
www.warnerpress.org

ISBN-13: 978-1-59317-562-7

Printed in the United States of America.
11 12 13 14 15 16 17 / EP / 10 9 8 7 6 5 4 3 2 1

This book is dedicated to the memory of my mother, Mrs. Gertrude Kinamore Moss-Holmes, who was a praying woman who taught me how to pray, and the meaning and value of prayer.

Thank you, Momma!

CONTENTS

INTRODUCTION

Prayer is a foundational part of my identity as a person, minister, and Christian disciple. When God called me into ministry, he spoke 1 Corinthians 11:5–6 in my spirit: "But every woman who prays or prophesies with her head uncovered dishonors her head, for that is one and the same as if her head were shaved. For if a woman is not covered, let her also be shorn. But if it is shameful for a woman to be shorn or shaved, let her be covered." I am a woman preacher and a prayer warrior, therefore I am shaved and covered. I am known as "the lady in the white prayer cap," and often people approach me on the streets to pray for them.

For the last thirty years, I have seen the effects of prayer in my life and in my ministry. I have long seen prayer as an important part of my faith walk with God. However, the events of November 8, 2008, taught me to pray in new ways. That was the night an arson fire destroyed our church building.

I knew that the only way our church would survive this ordeal was in and through prayer. My congregation looked to me for leadership and guidance, and the only thing I had to offer them was prayer. I had to teach and exemplify that we needed to seek God's face, remain a community of believers, and become a community of prayer warriors.

Make no mistake: I had always taught the people in my congregation to pray, led them in prayer, and emphasized the importance of prayer. And yet, the success of our ministry together fed a sense of complacency about prayer.

For eight wonderful years, I had been pastor at Bell's Chapel Church of God in Indianapolis. By the grace of God, our congregation had grown from just six persons to 175. The congregation had become a spiritual beacon on the corner of 42nd and Mitthoeffer, and God was doing great things. The church had opened a day care center that served more than one hundred children. We had launched several outreach ministries to the community. We regularly conducted preaching and teaching services in the men's and women's prisons. In these and many other ways, Bell's Chapel was ministering to the needy of our community. All of this came to a halt when fire destroyed our building.

The fire created many physical and logistical problems. Our community depended upon the church to care for their children, some for free or at reduced rates. Who would care for them now? The community depended on us for food, since our food pantry was open daily. Where would they get food now? Our doors were always open for prayer and counseling; people often came to the church for prayer and guidance. Where would they go now?

The fire created spiritual problems. One could accurately characterize Bell's Chapel as a congregation of "baby Christians"—that is, persons who were just learning who Christ is and how to live as disciples of Christ. Of our 175 constituents, 160 had made a first-time profession of faith and been baptized in the four years before the fire. These "baby Christians" were just learning how to pray and trust God, but they were not prepared to depend on God in the ways our circumstances now required. I wondered whether Bell's Chapel would continue to exist as a viable congregation. Without a physical church building, would the congregation draw closer to God or drift away? My key pastoral responsibility in this crisis was to ensure that the fire destroyed only the building, not the church.

The fire created financial problems. The church had become financially stable, with resources to help almost everyone who came to our doors for assistance, but now our financial viability was a big question mark. We had little financial reserves in the bank, so could we learn to "walk by faith and not by sight"?

The fire tested my own faith to the limits. There were times I wanted to give up and leave. Even so, God convicted me of my responsibility to stand firm and show that God was able to bring us through this ordeal victoriously. The stress of the fire created dissension and mistrust among our people. The fact that it was arson confronted us with the challenge of forgiveness—a challenge compounded when we fell victim to a fraudulent church fund-raiser in the early stages of rebuilding. I discovered repeatedly that I did not have the personal resources to address these needs, so I found myself turning to prayer more than ever before.

Jesus asserted that a place of worship is first of all a house of prayer (Matt 21:13). Here was the guiding vision for Bell's Chapel Church of God, to become God's covenant community, a community of prayer. We learned in the months following that fateful November night that prayer must be central to the life of our congregation.

Here I share with my colleagues in pastoral ministry what we learned together. Chapter One explores:

- The meaning of community and prayer
- The necessity of prayer and reasons to pray
- Methods of prayer, including how to pray, where to pray, when to pray, and what to pray about

Chapter Two reviews relevant literature from narrative theology and details a narrative frame of reference for pastoral care. Frequently, when teaching others to pray, I found myself drawing upon concepts of salvation story and sacred story. Indeed, my doctoral dissertation became a memoir of our congregation's experience with the church fire. Its title, "From Ashes to Beauty," encapsulated the ultimate meaning of our shared story. As Bell's Chapel moved through the overwhelming challenges it faced, through prayer and faith in our Lord and Savior Jesus Christ, God brought us from ashes to beauty. May you have a similar experience in becoming a community of prayer.

CHAPTER ONE
OUR NEED FOR PRAYER

"Behold, how good and how pleasant it is for brethren to dwell together in unity!" (Ps 133:1). Being together, being in community, is what God planned for humankind from the beginning, from Creation. Human community reflects the very nature of God, who lives in community as Father, Son, and Holy Spirit. Moreover, to be Christian is to be a person in community. Contrary to popular culture, which idolizes the individual, the church recognizes that living as a member of a community is essential.

> From the very beginning, God ordained that the making and the growth of community be the shared responsibility of all members of community. Community is deeply grounded in the nature of God. It flows from who God is because he is community, he created community. It is his gift of himself to humans. Therefore, the making of community may not be regarded as an optional decision for the Christians. It is a compelling and irrevocable necessity, a binding divine mandate for all believers at all times.[1]

The whole church has a common goal of being in communication and communion with God. Indeed, God draws us together for communion and fellowship with him. The church's ability to live as a community arises from God's empowerment

---

1. Bilezikian, *Community 101*, 27.

and assurance; for Jesus prayed, "Where two or three are gathered together in My name, I am there in the midst of them" (Matt 18:20).

Prayer is our primary means of coming together. When the earthly ministry of Jesus drew near to its tragic end, Jesus gathered his followers for one last meal together. The disciples feared an impending disaster, and Jesus knew already what it was: a cross on Mount Calvary. The moment was charged with emotion and heavy with sadness. Jesus opened his heart to them and spoke freely (John 13:16). Then he prayed (John 17). This high-priestly prayer of Jesus was the spiritual pinnacle of the night in which he was betrayed.

A few hours later, he would pray again to his Father in the relative seclusion of the Garden of Gethsemane. That Gethsemane prayer seemed to epitomize Jesus' prayer life, since the Gospels frequently portray him as praying in solitude. For example, Mark 1:35 says, "Now in the morning, having risen a long while before daylight, He went out and departed to a solitary place; and there He prayed."

However, the extended prayer of John 17 seems to occur in the context of community, as the disciples are gathered around the table with him. Dennis Kinlaw notes that the prayer emphasizes Jesus' concern for community. Here Jesus prays not only for his unity with the Father and his disciples but also for the unity of believers with one another in community.

Jesus underscores his concern for his disciples in the conclusion of his prayer to his Father (John 17:20–23). Jesus tells the Father that he is not praying simply for his eleven disciples, but for all who will believe on him in the future. The intimate relationship he is describing, which exists between him and his Father, is God's will not only for the original disciples, but also for every person who will ever believe. He prays that Christian believers will know oneness with God like the personal oneness the Son and the Father have. His prayer to the Father is that all believers may be *in* the Father and *in* the Son just as the Father is *in* the Son and the Son is *in* the Father. His purpose: "May they also be *in* us so that the world may believe that you have sent me" (v. 21, emphasis added). He concludes, "I have given them the glory that you gave me, that they may be one as we are one: I *in* them and you *in* me" (vv. 22–23, emphasis added).[2]

Apparently, Jesus is praying with the intention of being overheard. Why? "Although he was in close communion with the Father, he wanted to share his prayer with the disciples. So, he prayed audibly in their presence. They listened intently and registered his prayer in their memory."[3] With his disciples, Jesus formed a community of prayer.

Likewise, we should come together in community to pray. Once Jesus becomes the Lord of our lives, we are not alone, and we will never be alone. God tells Joshua in Deuteronomy 31:6, "Be strong and of good courage, do not fear nor be afraid of them; for the LORD your God, He is the One who goes with you. He will not leave you nor forsake you." Biblical witness speaks of spiritual community in familial terms (John 14:23). Scripture reveals God's character as one of faithfulness and loving care, like that of a father for his son (Luke 15:11–31); indeed, we have a Father who loves us more than we can begin to comprehend.

When the disciples asked Jesus to teach them to pray, he taught them a community form of prayer. Notice that he began with the words "Our Father" (Luke 11:2ff). He suggests that his Father, God, becomes our Father too, creating a community

---

2. Kinlaw, *Let's Start with Jesus*, 103.
3. Bilezikian, *Community 101*, 35.

with the Son and with us. "We address God," Barth points out, as "*our* Father," not in the singular but in the plural. God is not just "Father in general," but "*your* Father and *mine*, and therefore *our* Father: the Father of each individual who may invoke him thus." God is "the common Father of all who believe and of all who will come to believe him, so that they are all brothers and sisters as his children." The children of God who are "liberated for invocation of God as their Father exist in responsibility to him and therefore to his people and therefore to each of its many members."[4] So this is a universal, eternal community.

Paul's reflections on the church in 1 Corinthians 12 and Romans 12 suggest that the church is "the body of Christ," in other words, an organic whole comprising many diverse parts. C. Norman Kraus puts it this way: "The church is to call humans to change their ways and live in light of the new reality."[5] What better way to teach persons to "change their ways" than in communion with God and one another through prayer? Prayer is the result of change in situations and persons, but it also effects change in situations and persons.

We do not undertake prayer on our own but as a response to God's initiative in our lives. Songwriter William Walford penned the familiar lines:

> *Sweet hour of prayer, sweet hour of prayer*
> *that calls me from a world of care,*
> *and bids me at my Father's throne*
> *make all my wants and wishes known.*[6]

We pray because the Holy Spirit of God is already at work within us, inviting us to lay our petitions at the throne of the

---

4. Barth, *Prayer*, 119.
5. Kraus, *Community of the Spirit*, 102.
6. William Walford, "Sweet Hour of Prayer" (public domain).

heavenly King. Because prayer acknowledges the provenance of God's grace, it does not occur without the prior activity of the Spirit. As Scripture tells us, "The love of God has been poured out into our hearts by the Holy Spirit" (Rom 5:5). "The Spirit also helps in our weakness. For we do not know what we should pray for as we ought" (Rom 8:26).

And what are these petitions? For relief from death, we pray to God (Num 21:1–9). For stays of judgment, we pray to God (Deut 9:20, 26–29). For direction, we pray to God (Judg 1). For signs of divine favor, we pray to God (Judg 6; 2 Sam 5:19–25). For justification, we pray to God (Job 9). For protection against enemies, we pray to God (Ps 35). Every human need and aspiration is a matter for prayer. In all the circumstances of our lives, we can invoke God's presence through prayer.

Scripture instructs us to bring all our needs to God, and it pleases God when we do so. "The prayer of the upright is His delight" (Prov 15:8). We honor God as our Creator and Provider when we turn to him with our needs, both our own and those of the ones for whom we care (Luke 11:9–13). Cast "all your care upon Him, for He cares about you" (1 Peter 5:7). "Pray for one another, that you may be healed" (James 5:16).

Just as Scripture is the means by which God speaks to the Church, so prayer is the means by which the Church responds to God. Through Scripture God draws near to us. Through prayer, we draw near to God. That is to say, the Word of God is the means by which we receive God's redemptive presence and the way in which we acknowledge God's presence among us. In order to pray, the Church needs to hear God's Word. God's sovereign place for our lives comes to us by meditating on Scripture. Certainly, God may communicate with us through a medium outside the Word (e.g., through the kindness of a stranger, the beauty of the natural world, or the solace of music). But we cannot validate it as a message from God apart from its interpretation by means of Scripture.[7]

E. M. Bounds underlines the way in which Christian prayer is an expression of deep, intimate relationship with Christ. He writes:

> It is Jesus Christ, the Son of God, who commands us to pray, and it is He who puts Himself and all He has so fully in the answer. It is He who puts Himself at our service and answers our demands when we pray. Jesus puts Himself and the Father at our command in prayer; He promises to come directly into our lives and to work for our good. Also, He promises to answer the demands of two or more (community) believers who agree in prayer about any one thing. "If two of you shall agree on earth as touching anything that they shall ask, it shall be done for them of my Father which is in heaven" (Matthew 18:19).[8]

In other words, Jesus comes in community with God to call us to prayer, and we come in community with one another when we pray. Asserting that "the community of faith is indeed the climate and source of all prayer,"[9] Henri Nouwen reflects on ways that prayer demands of us things we cannot do as solitary individuals. Nouwen goes so far as to characterize prayer as a "superhuman task" when it comes to waiting on God. Temptations to impulsiveness, subterfuge, and self-deception require a community that enables us to discern God's presence even when God feels absent.

No one in modern theological circles has been more influential in understanding Christian community than Dietrich Bonhoeffer.

---

7. van Deusen Hunsinger, *Pray without Ceasing*, 28.

8. Bounds, *Weapon of Prayer*, 31.

9. Nouwen, *Reaching Out*, 118.

In *Life Together*, he points to the person of Jesus as the foundation of Christian community. "Christian community means community through and in Jesus Christ. On this presupposition rests everything that the Scripture provides in the way of directions and precepts for the communal life of Christians."[10] Bonhoeffer's definition of community stands in stark contrast to secular concepts of community in which the emphasis is strictly upon human connections. The word *community* usually connotes a way of being together that gives us a sense of belonging, but a community of prayer has a more transcendent purpose; it is a gathering of believers who seek to commune with Jesus Christ through prayer.

The Scriptures speak of prayer as urgent, necessary, and essential. Paul calls the church to "pray without ceasing" (1 Thess 5:17). James asserts that "the effective, fervent prayer of a righteous man avails much" (James 5:16). I believe that prayer will keep us from sinning; for Jesus teaches us to pray, "Do not lead us into temptation, But deliver us from the evil one" (Luke 11:4).

The word *prayer* is mentioned 114 times in the Bible,[11] with the first prayer being prayed in Genesis 4:26: "And as for Seth, to him also a son was born; and he named him Enosh. Then men began to call on the name of the LORD." Even in the earliest references of Scripture, we see that prayer is essential to expressing the spiritual aspect of our humanness.

Praying the Scriptures

When the Christian community finds itself in confusion about how to pray or what to say, we can always pray God's Word back to him. Praying the Scriptures is an historic practice of the church that draws directly from Jesus' example on the cross.

---

10. Bonhoeffer, *Life Together*, 24.
11. Strong, *Strong's Expanded Exhaustive Concordance* , 681.

As he was dying, Jesus prayed Psalm 22:1: "My God, My God, why have You forsaken Me?" Van Deusen Hunsinger reflects on this close connection between prayer and Scripture meditation. She suggests that Scripture even provides the words, images, and tone of prayer for the faith community.

> Whenever we meditate on Scripture, we are at the same time learning to pray. For the language that God uses forms in us the habits of mind needed for our response. Not only the church but also the people of Israel were trained to pray through words, images, and cadences of the Psalms, the prayerbook of the Bible. The Psalms offer the entire range of human response before God, teaching us to call upon God in trouble, to lament in times of trial, to praise God for life's blessings, to confess the sin that tempts us to despair, and to bow before God's majesty and holiness.[12]

Patton notes that prayer is a dialogue between God and humans in which people participate without fully understanding the conversation. The mystery of prayer arises from the deep, intimate relationship it embodies, but equally from the distance between the mind of God and human understanding. The fact that God responds to prayer, whether or not we fully understand what we are praying, confirms that the Holy Spirit is moving in the life of the community and in the lives of individuals who pray.[13]

Some persons in my congregation were afraid to pray publicly, lest they be embarrassed by what they said. These persons had to be taught that they were not talking to other worshipers but to God. They bowed their heads to demonstrate their humble submission to God. They closed their eyes to experience solitude

---

12. van Deusen Hunsinger, *Pray without Ceasing*, 45.
13. Patton, *If It Could Happen Here*, 51.

in the crowd, to shut out distractions and focus on God. Yet these postures also implied to them that prayer was a private matter, and their fear of praying in public betrayed this faulty theology of prayer. The pastoral challenge has been to move them from privatistic understandings of prayer to accept the fact that the whole community is praying when one member prays.

Martin Lloyd-Jones wrote: "Prayer is beyond any question the highest activity of the human soul. Man is at his greatest and highest when upon his knees he comes face to face with God."[14] Commentator J. Oswald Sanders adds:

No spiritual exercise is such a blending of complexity and simplicity. It is the simplest form of speech that infant lips can try, yet the sublimest strains that reach the Majesty on high. It is appropriate to the aged philosopher as to the little child. It is the ejaculation of a moment and the attitude of a lifetime. It is the expression of the rest of faith and of the fight of faith. It is an agony and an ecstasy. It is submissive and yet importunate. In the one moment it lays hold of God and binds the devil. It can be focused on a single objective and it can roam the world. It can be abject confession and rapt adoration. It invests puny man with a sort of omnipotence.[15]

Here Lloyd-Jones and Sanders articulate the paradoxical nature of prayer: Prayer is the grandest of human practices, yet it can be practiced by young children. There are no age limits on prayer and no guarantees that more experienced persons are more astute pray-ers. Prayer runs the gamut of emotions and motives. In many ways, these writers acknowledge that prayer is best known phenomenologically, that is, by experience. How

---

14. Lloyd-Jones, *Studies in the Sermon on the Mount*, [1]: 245.
15. Sanders, *Effective Prayer*, 7.

then might a pastor create opportunities for the faith community to have authentic experiences of prayer?

The essence of prayer is simply talking with God as we would with a beloved friend, without pretense. Yet it is at that very point that so many believers have trouble. Peter Wagner suggests in *Churches That Pray* that difficulties in the practice of prayer are a matter of spiritual warfare.[16] Because communion with God is so vital and prayer so effective in the fulfillment of God's plan, our spiritual enemy attempts constantly to introduce errors into our understanding of and commitment to prayer. Henri Nouwen also alludes to spiritual opposition in prayer when he says, "Praying, if it is anything more than a narcissistic self-complaint, involves someone else, another who is not just me. Praying then means creating distance and God's answer is given in the praying act."[17]

Prayer is not offered so that God can find out what we need, because Jesus tells us, "Your Father knows the things you have need of before you ask Him" (Matt 6:8). Rather, prayer expresses our trust in God and is a means whereby our trust in him can increase. In fact, the primary emphasis of the Bible's teaching on prayer is that we are to pray with faith, that is, trust or dependence on God. God, our Creator, delights in being trusted by us as his creatures, for an attitude of dependence is most appropriate to the Creator-creature relationship.

Richard Foster speaks of prayer as a "conversion of the heart." Beginning with the notion of what he refers to as "simple prayer," he suggests that building a trust relationship with God begins very simply by talking to God about whatever is on one's mind. Even if we are self-absorbed at the beginning, prayer places us in conversation with God and offers the opportunity of turning upward to God. Foster reflects that at some

---

16. Wagner, *Churches That Pray*, 133–37.
17. Nouwen, *Intimacy*, 46.

point in our growth in prayer, a shift in our center of gravity occurs: "We pass from thinking of God as part of our life to the realization that we are part of his life."[18]

We may regard prayer with the utmost respect yet find that our own practice lacks purpose and vitality, so we don't spend time with God as we know we should. While there are many reasons Christians struggle to pray, I believe Lloyd-Jones identifies a significant barrier:

> It is the highest activity of the human soul, and therefore it is at the same time the ultimate test of a man's true spiritual condition. There is nothing that tells the truth about us as Christian people so much as our prayer life. . . . Ultimately, therefore, a man discovers the real condition of his spiritual life when he exams himself in private, when he is alone with God...And have we not all known what it is to find that, somehow, we have less to say to God when we are alone than when we are in the presence of others? It should not be so; but it often is. So that it is when we have left the realm of activities and outward dealings with other people and are alone with God that we really know where we stand in a spiritual sense.[19]

Prayer is a believer's normal response to pressure. Seldom do we seriously come to God just to thank him, but our prayers become most sincere in times of trouble, in times of stress when we have to cry out, lie prostrate, and groan before him. After the fire at Bell's Chapel, some of our members just began to groan because they could not verbalize their deepest feelings to God. Out of faith or human desperation, we Christians believe that when we talk with God during crisis, God will provide

---

18. Foster *Prayer*, 14–15.
19. Lloyd-Jones, *Studies in the Sermon on the Mount*, [1]: 45.

answers, solace, and consolation. However, the Bible suggests that prayer is a strategy of change, not simply a reaction to overwhelming circumstances.

Acts 12:1–19 relates the story of Peter's miraculous deliverance from prison as an answer to the prayers of the faith community. This account also describes the ironic experience of answered prayer. When Peter is freed and appears at the door of the congregation's prayer meeting, they say to Rhoda (the girl reporting that he has arrived), "You are out of your mind!" (Acts 12:15 NRSV). Earnest prayer, whether for change of a miraculous or more garden-variety nature, requires the eyes of faith to see it answered.

Over and over in Scripture, God's people witness to the power of prayer in their lives. "I called on the LORD in distress" (Ps 118:5). "In the day of my trouble I sought the Lord" (Ps 77:2). The psalmist often reminds us that prayer is instinctive in times of sorrow and trouble. Even so, doesn't Scripture commend prayer at all times? Does not the apostle Paul say, "But in everything by prayer and supplication, with thanksgiving, let your requests be made known to God" (Phil 4:6)?

What is prayer? Earlier, we described it simply as communication with God, but Charles Spurgeon offers a more eloquent description of prayer:

> An approach of the soul by the Spirit of God to the throne of God. It is not the utterance of words, it is not alone the feeling of desires, but it is the advance of the desires to God, the spiritual approach of our nature toward the Lord our God. True prayer is neither a mere mental exercise nor a vocal performance. It is far deeper than that, it is spiritual transaction with the Creator of heaven and earth. God is a Spirit unseen of mortal eye and only to be perceived by the inner man. Our spirit within us, begotten by the Holy Ghost at our regeneration, discerns the Great Spirit,

communes with Him, presents to Him its request, and receives from Him answers of peace.[20]

Spurgeon sees prayer as both communication and communion with God. His comment raises practical questions. Does God speak to us through prayer? Are we actually in communion with God when we pray?

Walter Elwell reflects that what we believe is evidenced by how we live our faith. He describes prayer as the means by which the Holy Spirit illumines the Word or Wisdom of God (Gk. *Logos*) and applies it to the human heart. He draws upon John Calvin's characterization of prayer as "the soul of faith," that is, the practice that brings life to faith. For Elwell, prayer is a two-way street, a conversation with God in which both parties speak from the heart.[21]

True prayer is not just a mental exercise or a vocal performance, but it is the outpouring of one's soul to a holy God with anticipation and expectation. Prayer is the heart of spirituality and therefore has priority over other areas of the spiritual life. Dallas Willard asserts in *Hearing God* that

> the biblical record always presents the relationship between God and the believer as more like a friendship or family tie than like merely one person's arranging to take care of the needs of another. If we pass before our minds that startling array of biblical personalities from Adam to the apostles Paul and John we behold the millennia-long saga of God's invading human personality and history on a one-to-one basis.[22]

---

20. Spurgeon, *Power of Prayer*, 15.
21. Elwell, *Evangelical Dictionary of Theology*, 866.
22. Willard, *Hearing God*, 23.

Prayer is a universal phenomenon, firmly rooted in the human condition. As Barth aptly notes, prayer is an expression of our "incurable God-sickness."[23]

We noted earlier that prayer is not only communication with God but also *communion* with God, i.e., simply being in the presence of God. Elwell comments, "True prayer, in the prophetic or biblical sense, bursts through all forms and techniques. This is because it has its basis in the Spirit of God, who cannot be encased in a sacramental box or a ritualistic formula."[24]

Biblical prayer is crying to God out of the depths; it is the pouring out of the soul before God. "But Hannah answered and said, 'No, my lord, I am a woman of sorrowful spirit. I have drunk neither wine nor intoxicating drink, but have poured out my soul before the LORD'" (1 Sam 1:15). "O LORD, God of my salvation, I have cried out day and night before You. Let my prayer come before You; Incline Your ear to my cry" (Ps 88:1–2). Jesus Christ, "in the days of His flesh…offered up prayers and supplications, with vehement cries and tears to Him who was able to save Him from death, and was heard because of His godly fear" (Heb 5:7). These were prayers uttered by persons spontaneously crying to God from the depths of their hearts.

Bradley Holt describes prayer in relational terms with an emphasis on the holistic nature of prayer. Asserting that prayer is more than asking God for what we need and want, Holt offers two acrostics for styles of prayer that include the sweep of communication with God. In the acronym ACTS, he suggests that prayer involves at least four movements:

Adoration
Confession

---

23. Barth, *Prayer*, 815.
24. Elwell, *Evangelical Dictionary of Theology*, 867.

Thanksgiving
Supplication

The style outlined by the PRAY acrostic includes:

Praise
Repent
Ask
Yield

Holt also suggests that prayer can focus more on listening than speaking to God. It may be merely "a wordless listening in a loving presence."[25] More often, prayer involves both speaking to God and listening for God to speak to us.

Prayer indeed brings us consciously into the presence of God, who loves us and delights in fellowship with us. In authentic prayer, one comes in the wholeness of character to relate to God as a person, in the wholeness of his character. Hence, all that we think or feel about God comes to expression in our prayer.

Willard observes that when we pray, God's voice speaks into our souls. He writes:

> The voice of God speaking in our souls also bears within itself a characteristic spirit. It is a spirit of exalted peacefulness and confidence, of joy, of sweet reasonableness and of goodwill. It is, in short, the spirit of Jesus, and by that phrase I refer to the overall tone and internal dynamics of his personal life as a whole. Those who had seen Jesus had truly seen the Father, who shared the same Spirit. It is this Spirit that marks the voice of God in our hearts. Any word that bears an opposite spirit most surely is not the voice of

---

25. Holt, *Thirsty for God*, 19.

God. And because his voice bears authority within itself, it does not need to be loud or hysterical.[26]

God's voice often comes in surprising ways. It may seem a still small voice like that heard by the prophet Elijah. First Kings 19 says that Elijah was depressed because he felt alone and persons were seeking to take his life. He desperately needed to hear from God. "Then [God] said, 'Go out, and stand on the mountain before the LORD.' And behold, the LORD passed by, and a great and strong wind tore into the mountains and broke the rocks in pieces before the LORD, but the LORD was not in the wind; and after the wind an earthquake, but the LORD was not in the earthquake; and after the earthquake a fire, but the LORD was not in the fire; and after the fire a still small voice." Often one looks for God to speak boldly, as with thunder from heaven, while God may choose to speak in the recesses of our minds as with a "still small voice."

As Natural as Breathing

Paul encourages the church at Thessalonica to "pray without ceasing" (1 Thess 5:17). Here prayer seems analogous to breathing. Paul directs Christians to develop a "reflex" of prayer, something that comes naturally, automatically, without conscious thought. One does not have to think about breathing, because the atmosphere exerts pressure on the lungs and forces a person to breathe. That is why it is more difficult to hold your breath than to breathe. Similarly, when one is born into the family of God, that person enters into a spiritual atmosphere wherein God's presence and grace exert a pressure or influence on life. Prayer is the normal response to that pressure. As believers, we

---

26. Willard, *Hearing God*, 177.

have entered the divine atmosphere, so it is only natural to breathe the air of prayer. In a real sense, the breath of prayer is necessary for our survival.

Unfortunately, many believers hold their spiritual "breath" for long periods, thinking that brief moments with God are sufficient to allow them to survive. Why is this? For some, ignorance about the necessity of prayer leaves them dependent on the artificial respiration of secular assumptions. Others are not prepared for the level of intimacy with God that prayer demands. However, every believer must be continually in the presence of God, constantly breathing in God's Spirit to be fully functional.

How can prayer be a part of everyday life in the Christian community? Jesus instructs disciples to petition God for our daily bread. (How can one petition God for daily bread if we are not communicating with him on a daily basis?) Intimidating though it may be, discipleship requires us to be in daily contact with the One sitting on the throne of grace.

This is why Wagner describes prayer as "the moment before God." "The moment before God can be something more than mere custom or habit. If one prays only out of habit, the tendency is to engage in a performance, what theologians refer to as 'rhetoric prayer.'"[27] When we are conscious of the power and majesty of God, we cannot take this moment for granted. The mature life of prayer is an intentional pattern in which one plans daily for such wholly present moments. It is for such moments that the love of God seeks us.

In Matthew 6: 5–15, Jesus warns against certain forms of prayer that were popular in his time:

- *Performance prayers* given in a manner and venue designed to attract attention (Matt 6:5).

---

27. Wagner, *Churches That Pray*, 18–20.

- *Stylistic prayers* that rely on magical formulae or rituals of "babbling," assaulting God with many words (Matt 6:7).
- *Shallow prayers* that seek reconciliation with God while remaining in unforgiveness, bitterness, and resentment toward one's neighbor (Matt 6:12, 14–15).

In other words, our prayers do not have to be long or formal in order to be genuine. A prayer may be as short and simple as taking a breath. For example, "Thank you, God"; "Lord, have mercy"; "Lord, help me"; Lord, I need your Spirit"; "Come right now, Jesus." These simple prayers keep the lines of communication open between us and God. We may begin to utter breath prayers, then sentence prayers, then paragraph prayers, and so forth. But whatever forms they may take, prayer must be a part of our daily routine.

John MacArthur observes that the natural, daily nature of prayer does not preclude the need for passion and devotion in prayer. He underscores the fact that prayer remains an urgent calling in one's life, despite its habitual nature. To pray is to stay alert to God's voice and persevere in God's will, as we are told in Colossians 4:2: "Devote yourselves to prayer, keeping alert in it" (NRSV). The apostle Paul warned the Ephesians to "be watchful...with all perseverance and supplication" as they prayed (6:18).[28]

Through prayer God gives peace, which is one reason even self-sufficient types fall on their knees and pour out their hearts to God. One prays because, by intuition or experience, one understands that perfect peace comes only through relating with the Peacemaker.

But there is another reason people are drawn to prayer: They know that God's power flows primarily to people who

---

28. MacArthur, *Alone with God*, 24.

pray. God's power can change circumstances and relationships; it can help one face life's daily struggles. That power can heal psychological and physical problems, remove marital obstructions, and meet financial needs.

Jesus' earthly ministry was brief, barely three years long, yet he spent much of that time in prayer. The Gospels report that Jesus habitually rose early in the morning, often before daybreak, to commune with his Father (Luke 4:42). In the evening, Jesus would frequently go to some quiet place to pray, usually alone (John 8:1). Prayer was the spiritual air that Jesus breathed every day of his earthly life. He practiced an unending communion between himself and the Father (John 11:40–42).

Jesus himself prayed what Bible commentators refer to as the "High Priestly Prayer" in John 17, where he served as the mighty Intercessor, pouring out his heart to the Father. Christ offered this prayer on the night in which he was betrayed, mere hours before the terrible ordeal of his crucifixion. We might call this the true "Lord's Prayer." Here Jesus moved in three distinct circles: He prayed for himself (vv 1–8), he prayed for his own (vv 9–19), and he prayed for the world (vv 20–26). This should also be the prayer pattern for the church: We ought to pray for the continuation of the church, for the members of our congregation, and for the world.

Jesus urged his disciples to "watch therefore, and pray always that you may be counted worthy to escape all these things that will come to pass, and to stand before the Son of Man" (Luke 21:36). The early church carried on his commitment to continual, unceasing prayer. Even before the Day of Pentecost, the twelve disciples gathered in the upper room and "continued with one accord in prayer and supplication" (Acts 1:14). That did not change even when three thousand were added to their number on the Day of Pentecost (Acts 2:41). When the church grew to the point that the apostles had to restructure its order of ministry, so that the work of ministry could be accomplished more effectively, they said, "We will give ourselves continually to prayer and to the ministry of the word" (Acts 6:4).

Throughout his life, the apostle Paul exemplified this commitment to prayer. In the benedictions to many of his epistles, we find that praying for his fellow believers was his daily practice. To the Roman believers, he said, "God is my witness...that without ceasing I make mention of you always in my prayers, making request" (Rom 1:9–10; cf 1 Cor 1:4; Eph 5:20; Phil 1:4; Col 1:3; 1 Thess 1:2; 2 Thess 1:3, 11; Philem 4).

Christian prayer is possible because Jesus Christ mediates between God and us (Heb 7:25). Christians can have communion with God only because Christ's atonement has been accomplished. As Jesus himself declared, "No one comes to the Father except through Me" (John 14:6b).

Theologically speaking, prayer and providence go hand in hand. However, thoughtful Christians often wonder about the role of prayer in God's providence. Millard Erickson states, "The dilemma stems from the question of what prayer really accomplishes." In other words, can one change God's mind through prayer? Erickson frames his theology of prayer in relational terms that affirm God's sovereignty as well as the value of prayer. He envisions God's work in the world as a mysterious partnership between God and human beings in which God invites us to have a say in what God will do. Asserting that prayer is "more than self-stimulation," Erickson proposes that prayer is a way of bringing the collective will of the people into alignment with the will of God. This alignment involves not only pulling in the same direction as God, but also accepting the goodness and superiority of God's will when our desires differ from God's plan.[29]

Jesus' teachings presuppose that prayer is necessary. He begins a discourse on prayer with the words, "And when you

---

29. Erickson, *Christian Theology*, 405.

pray..." (Matt 6:5). Notice that Jesus does not say, "*If* you pray," but, "*When* you pray." His comment implies that prayer is a necessary and normal action for his followers. This suggests a surprising definition of "normal": No one is truly normal who does not pray. The Christian who does not take time regularly to have communion with God through prayer is not at his/her best. Through prayer, God intervenes in the affairs of this earth. God has given human beings dominion over the earth, so he will not interfere in earthly affairs unless he is invited. Prayer is the primary way the faith community can invite God to enter into its life.

In Jonah 1:6, God addresses Jonah's anxious flight from God. "What do you mean, sleeper? Arise, call upon your God." Beyond Jonah's immediate situation in a tempest, I believe this text is an exhortation to the whole faith community.

Along the same vein, Charles Spurgeon insists that God yearns for people to pray in times of weakness. Spurgeon writes, "God understands what heavy hearts we have sometimes, especially when we are under a sense of sin."[30] The temptation is to give up or, as Spurgeon suggests, to give in to the temptation of despair. Under the pressure of guilt and shame, we are tempted to assume that our bad behavior has so displeased God that he will refuse to listen to our prayer. However, Spurgeon reminds us that we find reassurance of God's mercy through prayer, providing the strength to come against the lies of Satan.

Prayer is also the means of obtaining God's guidance and aid in a number of difficult situations. Christians pray in preparation for major decisions (Luke 6:12–13); to overcome demonic barriers (Matt 17:14–21); to gather workers for the spiritual harvest (Luke 10:2); to gain strength to overcome temptation (Matt 26:41); and to obtain the means of strengthening others spiritually (Eph 6:18–19).

---

30. Spurgeon, *Power of Prayer*, 49.

When we come to God with our specific requests, the Scriptures promise that our prayers are not in vain, even if we do not receive specifically what we asked for (Matt 6:6; Rom 8:26–27). The Bible promises that when believers ask for things that are in accordance with God's will, God will grant their requests (1 John 5:14–15).

Even so, God's timing in answer to prayer can be particularly difficult to discern and accept. Sometimes God delays in answering for our benefit. In these situations, we are to be diligent and persistent in prayer (Matt 7:7; Luke 18:1–8), realizing that prayer is not a means of getting God to do the will of his people on earth, but rather a means of getting his will done on earth. However long God's response may take, and whatever form it might take, let us remember that God's infinite wisdom far exceeds our own. Henri Nouwen asserts in his book *Reaching Out* that

> we cannot force God into a relationship. God comes to us on his own initiative, and no discipline, effort or ascetic practice can make him come. All mystics stress with an impressive unanimity that prayer is "grace," that is, a free gift from God, to which we can only respond with gratitude.[31]

Rather than something attainable only by holy men and women secluded from society, prayer allows all believers to develop a close relationship with God. God welcomes prayers and desires to meet the needs of those who pray. To pray is to trust God with one's most precious thoughts and concerns. Again, we see that prayer is not just a means for securing things we need, but it is also a transforming and intimate connection to God.

Through prayer, we express our dependency upon the almighty God. Gilbert Stafford writes:

---

31. Nouwen, *Reaching Out*, 93.

The Christian's deepest relationship with God, strongest link with others, and greatest contribution to the upbuilding of the body of Christ is prayer. It is our way of being connected to God for the good of the world; it is God's design for divine-human partnership; it is the divine way for us to participate in heavenly plans for earthly purposes. Prayer is that activity by which we live up to our full potential as creatures in the image of God. As Eugene Peterson puts it: "The primary use of prayer is not for expressing ourselves, but in becoming ourselves."[32]

In order for one to build relationship with God, one must talk with God and listen for God to respond. One can never truly know God without communicating directly with him.

Prayer might be characterized as the greatest expression of our faith. The writer of Hebrews defines faith as "the substance of things hoped for, the evidence of things not seen" (Heb 11:1). Is not that what prayer is, talking to God, who is not seen, and expecting something to happen?

Although God is unseen, some find it useful to form a visualization of God as they pray. Some see God as sitting on a throne, high and lifted up, with humans bowing before him. Some see God as a woman, a mother enfolding us in her arms. Some see God as their "homey," or best buddy, with whom they are having a heart-to-heart conversation. Some see God as a father figure whom they approach timidly. Perhaps inevitably, to pray is to place in our minds images of God, inadequate and defective though they may be.

---

32. Stafford, *Theology for Disciples*, 411.

CHAPTER TWO

APPROACHES TO PRAYER

How are Christians to pray? Much of the literature about prayer is devoted to this question: Is there a right way to pray?

First of all, Scripture tells us, God does not want us to pile up impressive phrases. God does not want us to use words without thinking about their meaning. "And when you pray, do not use vain repetitions as the heathen do. For they think that they will be heard for their many words" (Matt 6:7). God expects us to talk to him as we might a friend or father—authentically, reverently, personally, earnestly. We need to focus outward, discerning who God is and what he expects of us, at least as much as we focus on things that concern us.

Prayer Begins with Praise

The pattern of prayer Jesus taught his disciples suggests that prayer begins with praise. In Luke 11:2 he says, "When you pray, say: Our Father in heaven, Hallowed be Your name." The word *hallowed* in Greek is *hagiazo*, which means holy, sanctified. J. C. Ryle reflects that to pray in God's name is to ask that God's character, represented in God's name, might be seen through the fabric of our lives. Invoking God's name in prayer is not some sort of magical thinking, but a way of honoring and glorifying God.[1]

---

1. Ryle, *Luke*, 151.

The name of God is to be praised and hallowed. To pray "Hallowed be Your name" is to set apart God in one's mind to be praised and adored. Keeping praise and reverence for God as the foundation of prayer prevents prayer from becoming a wish list for a divine Santa Claus.

John Calvin put it this way: "That God's name should be hallowed is to say that God should have His own honor of which He is so worthy, so that men should never think or speak of Him without the greatest veneration. This may sound like a strictly 'religious' activity, but it isn't."[2]

Francis Reinberger characterizes praise in prayer as "self-forgetful." He suggests that praising God is not an attempt to manipulate God. Rather, praise arises from the realization of God's greatness and good character. In this sense, praise of God is an overflow from gratitude for God's provision and wonder at the beauty and majesty of creation.[3]

In the context of praise to God, one makes supplications, requests of God. Truly, nothing is too big for God to handle or too small for God to have an interest. To pray authentically is to tell God—the One you adore and revere above all others—the deep desires of your heart. It may help to order our thoughts if we organize our requests into categories, such as ministry, people, family, and personal needs. Likewise, maintaining a prayer journal can be a means for understanding more clearly how we pray and how God is working. Prayer journals provide the opportunity to go back after a few weeks, to reread the list of prayers, and reflect on the larger pattern of interaction with God around our perceived needs. To systematically reflect on God's answers to prayer is to discover God's faithfulness, which gives us even more reason to praise him.

---

2. Jeremiah, *Prayer*, 90.
3. Reinberger, *How to Pray*, 11.

What We Can Learn from Children

Ironically, children can help adults learn to pray. The best way to learn how to pray is to begin praying, just as a child first learns to talk by listening to people and responding spontaneously to them. The child does not consciously make up his mind to talk. The speaking of another person prompts the child to talk, as communication from our heavenly Father prompts us to pray.

Children show us how to express authentic feelings in a plainspoken way. Daniel Akin offers the example of a child's praying:

> One little five-year-old knelt down with his mother for his bedtime prayers. He folded his hands, closed his eyes, and asked God to bless the ones he loved. At the end, he opened his eyes, looked upward, and with a grin on his face said, "And God, we'll have fun again tomorrow." In an ironic way, the most effective and honest prayers are also the simplest. Sometimes small children can teach us a great deal about a natural religious life. That was a true statement of the boy's feelings, of joy over a good day now ending and faith that the next day would be just as good. He did not think it all out, he felt good and he told God how he felt.[4]

This young boy was natural with his prayers; we should be just as natural with ours.

When Prayer Is Awkward

Someone who has had a broken leg knows the helpless feeling of not being able to walk. The doctor sets the bones in the leg,

---

4. Akin, *Theology for the Church*, 44.

puts on a cast, and takes good care of the patient so that the leg heals properly. However, medical treatment alone will not guarantee that the patient will walk again. One has to want to walk for the leg to regain strength and usability. So the patient has to shuffle, stumble, and sometimes painfully force the leg to move until he can resume walking normally. One learns to walk again only by walking.

In an analogous way, one learns to pray by praying—stumbling, halting, and imperfect though the efforts may be. There is no right or wrong way to pray. Whatever is felt in the heart when one bows before God is what should be uttered to God. MacArthur writes:

> The Word of God makes clear that God wanted to hear the prayers of the people. Psalm 65:2 says, "O Thou who dost hear prayer, to Thee all men come." The Midrash, a Jewish commentary on portions of the Old Testament, says this about two people speaking at the same time, but with God it is not so. "All pray before Him, and He understands and receives all their prayers" (*Rabbah* 21.4). Men may become tired of listening to people, but God's ears are never satiated—He is never wearied by men's prayers.[5]

Let us not forget that God is the enabling and empowering party in prayer. When our prayers seem so inadequate and poorly articulated, God still sustains the conversation. Akin reflects that prayer is one of the many forms of grace that come into our lives through the intercession of the Holy Spirit. Akin suggests that the very ability to start praying is a gift of God, and it is multiplied in gifts of perseverance and guidance in prayer as the Holy Spirit works within us.[6]

---

5. MacArthur, *Alone with God*, 37.
6. Akin, *Theology for the Church*, 290.

Learning to Converse with God

Whether we pray aloud or silently, the language and manner-isms of prayer are a natural expression of who we are. In other words, we do not need to use rarified theological language to pray. Prayer is like talking with a very special friend. This means sharing our feelings as well as thoughts with God in a way that is normal and natural.

Most people need guidance to practice the art of conversa-tion with God. Talking with someone who is out of reach of the senses is a difficult assignment. We are accustomed to dealing with objects or persons whom we can see or hear or feel or smell. It is human to feel more at ease with entities that are concrete and substantial; abstract things are more difficult. Hope must underlie our prayers to God. We must pray hoping God is there, hoping God is listening, and hoping God will answer. Many people are unaccustomed to this, so they feel fearful and anxious in prayer. These negative emotional reactions stand in contrast with the biblical descriptions of prayer as a place of rest and re-freshment. To pray is to rest in God (Ps 46:10).

Centering Prayer

Daily life is filled with activities and tensions that cause our thoughts and feelings to move at a rapid, often hectic, pace. Trying to pray in such a distracted state of mind is discourag-ing. One should prepare for meeting with God by letting go of worries and centering one's thoughts and emotions. The ancient practice of centering prayer provides us a means toward this end. Centering prayer begins with finding a quiet space where one will not be interrupted. One then turns his attention to his breathing, allowing the breath to deepen and slow in rhythm. At the same time, one seeks to empty the mind of worrisome preoccupations, allowing the thoughts to float away. The concept here is not to rush into thinking about God but rather to create a space into which God might speak and be heard.

Centering prayer can be practiced in a wide variety of settings with minimal distractions. It may be in the quiet of one's bedroom, under a shady tree by a river, on a park bench along a busy city boulevard, or in the coolness of an empty church sanctuary. When relaxed, one thinks more sharply, sees more clearly, and feels more confident. Most of all, relaxation allows us to hear and see in new ways. We can focus on God, occupied only by our conversation and our communion with him.

Centering prayer prepares us to receive the gift of contemplative prayer, in which we experience God's presence within us, closer than our own breathing, our thinking, or our consciousness itself. Contemplative prayer is a discipline that fosters a relationship of unparalleled intimacy with God.

Centering prayer is not meant to replace other kinds of prayer. Rather, it adds depth of meaning to all prayer and facilitates our movement from more active modes of prayer—verbal, mental, or affective prayer—into a receptive prayer of resting in God. Centering prayer moves beyond conversation with God to communion with him.

Basil Pennington, one of the best-known proponents of the centering prayer technique, has delineated these guidelines for centering prayer:[7]

- Sit comfortably with your eyes closed, relax and quiet yourself. Be in love and faith to God.
- Choose a sacred word that best supports your sincere intention to be in the Lord's presence and open to His divine action within you (i.e., "Jesus," "Lord," "God," "Savior," "Abba," "Divine," "Shalom," "Spirit," "Love," etc.).

---

7. Pennington, *Centering Prayer*, 222.

- Let that word be gently present as your symbol of your sincere intention to be in the Lord's presence and open to His divine action within you.
- Whenever you become aware of anything (thoughts, feelings, perceptions, images, associations, etc.), simply return to your sacred word, your anchor.

Ideally, such prayer will reach a point where the person praying is no longer engaged in his or her own thoughts, but only conscious of the divine presence.

For those who still struggle with distraction in prayer, additional steps may be in order. Try writing down the distractions as they come to mind. Some of us find ourselves distracted from prayer because we think about all the things we need to do that day. If we keep paper and pen close by, so we can write down each task as it comes to mind, we can allow ourselves to forget about it until later. If still unable to stop thinking about a particular concern, we can take it to God in prayer. Distractions cannot prevent us from praying if we make the distractions themselves a matter of prayer.

When to Pray

What are the best times for us to pray? Reinberger believes prayer is organic and could occur at all times of day and night in keeping with the flow of life. Ironically, the effort to follow a strict schedule for prayer might hinder rather than help our prayer relationship with God. Instead, Reinberger suggests that we conceive of prayer as a running conversation with a friend. Friends talk when they feel moved, as often or sporadically as life might dictate.[8]

---

8. Reinberger, *How to Pray*, 53.

Daniel prayed three times a day—evening, morning, and noon. "Now when Daniel knew that the writing was signed, he went home. And in his upper room, with his windows open toward Jerusalem, he knelt down on his knees three times that day, and prayed and gave thanks before his God, as was his custom since early days" (Dan 6:10). Even so, the New Testament prayer mandate is more thoroughgoing. According to Paul, Christians are to pray all the time, without ceasing, and anywhere (1 Thess 5:17; 1 Tim 2:8).

Where is the best place to pray? Any place is suitable for prayer. Jesus prayed in the temple and the synagogue. He prayed on top of a mountain and in homes where he stayed. He prayed in a garden. So may we. One can talk with God anytime and anywhere. These are moments of inward communion.

John Killinger reflects on prayer as silence. In his estimation, prayer is entering into God's presence without the need to have something to say. He calls prayer "listening to the silence," and suggests that one hears in prayer a countercultural and counterintuitive word. Here one confronts the false images of the world, the pettiness of one's ambitions, and the groundless fears that control life. Beyond these faulty worldviews, God speaks the reality of grace into the lives of those who pray. Grace appears as spiritual fruit—love, joy, peace, and patience.[9]

Similarly, R. A. Torrey reflects on the secret nature of prayer. He cautions us against praying to an audience, the ultimate distraction in prayer. Instead, Torrey commends prayer in which one intentionally withdraws from the world to be "shut in alone with God." For him, having a secret place to meet with God is essential to a vital, growing prayer life.[10]

Every Christian should be a continuing student of the experience of prayer. Prayer not only permits us communion

---

9. Killinger, *Prayer*, 33.
10. Torrey, *What the Bible Teaches*, 395.

with God, it has consequences. Prayer lifts the darkness from the eyes of the inner man and grants undefeatable strength in times of stress and strain. Prayer helps us sustain morals, teaches us to control and use our possessions with wisdom, and reveals how to handle ourselves to the glory of God. By prayer we rise above confusion, escape hazards and pitfalls, achieve new insights, and strengthen our hold upon eternal values. In prayer at its best, we find the open vistas of spiritual splendor. One can harness the power of prayer into service for life. We may think we control prayer as a personal exercise, but prayer exerts control on us, extending a divine call to our souls. Prayer opens us to that which is beyond naming and sends us back into the outer world with a staggering fullness of glory. When we truly pray, we learn that life is not a problem but a purpose.

"Prayer is the key to confidence, boldness, and revival for the individual Christian and for the church as a whole," writes Donald Bloesch. Quoting Lorenzo Scupoli, he continues further:

> Every thought which discourages and hinders thee from increasing in love and confidence towards God is a messenger of hell...Thou must drive it away, and neither admit it nor give it a hearing. For the office of the Holy Spirit is none other than always and on all occasions to unite the soul more and more closely to God, enkindling and inflaming it with His sweet love, and inspiring it with fresh confidence. [11]

When we begin learning to pray with all our heart, prayer overflows into more of our lives. As our relationship with God deepens, that becomes easier to do.

---

11. Bloesch, *Struggle of Prayer*, 149.

What should Christians pray about? The Scriptures commend our prayer about everything. All through Scripture, we find people uttering prayers to God for numerous things:

- In Genesis 25, Isaac prays for his barren wife, Rebekah, and she conceives a child (Gen 25:19–23).
- Moses prays for a new leader, who becomes Joshua (Num 27:15–17).
- In Judges the children of Israel pray for direction (Judg 1:1).
- Manoah prays for his unborn child, asking for guidance in training his child (Judg 13:12).
- The barren Hannah, without words, prays for a child and she conceives and gives birth to Samuel (1 Sam 1:9–13).
- Again in 1 Samuel, Samuel prays for "a king to judge us" for the children of Israel, and David is anointed King (1 Sam 8:6).
- David prays for his sick child (2 Sam 12:16).
- Ezra prays a prayer of thanksgiving for the beautifying of the house of the Lord (Ezra 7:27–28).
- Jonah prays for release from hell and is released (Jonah 2:1–9).
- In Matthew the leper prays to Jesus to be made clean and he is cleansed (Matt 8:1–4).
- Jesus prays at the grave of Lazarus and Lazarus comes forth from the dead (John 11:41–42).

All through the Bible, prayers are uttered to God about every sort of issue that concerns the human heart. If something matters to human beings, it matters to God. This is why Paul exhorts us, "In everything by prayer and supplication, with thanksgiving, let your request be made known to God; and the peace of God, which surpasses all understanding, will guard your hearts and minds through Christ Jesus" (Phil 4:6–7). We who follow Christ should pray about everything!

Elwell challenges the church to remember that prayer has an outward movement: the transformation of the world. By praying that God's will be done on earth, the church commits itself to making this prayer a reality. In a profound sense, prayer asserts that God's purposes are the first priority beyond any person's or any community's agenda.[12]

Perhaps the greatest challenge in prayer is to persevere. Undoubtedly, there will be times that God does not answer prayer right away, and so we have to persevere in prayer. This means to be steadfast, to continue despite difficulty and opposition. A good example of this is found in the gospel of Luke in the parable of the persistent widow. Jesus tells this story of a woman who went to a judge to get justice. "And he would not for a while; but afterward he said within himself... 'lest by her continual coming she weary me'" (Luke 18:4–5). Because of her persistence, she got what she wanted. Jesus commends this kind of persistent, active seeking after God's will and intervention. "Ask, and it will be given to you; seek, and you will find; knock, and it will be opened to you" (Matt 7:7). He does not imply that we are to ask once, seek once, or knock once; rather, we are to keep on asking, keep on seeking, and keep on knocking. An important function of perseverance in prayer is building clarity and commitment in the person who is praying. Over time, persistent prayer helps us become sure of what we are seeking from God, what we are hoping to find, and what obstacle we are knocking upon, so that it may be opened.

Most persons who have ever prayed wonder what form God's answer may take. When one goes to God in prayer, there is not a *carte blanche* guarantee that God will answer in the manner and timing one desires. God answers prayers in three

---

12. Elwell, *Evangelical Dictionary of Theology*, 867.

essential ways: yes, no, and wait. Sometimes the matter of our prayer is resolved right away; that is God saying yes. At other times, God does not respond in an obvious way, and we may call the result "unanswered prayer" when, in reality, God's answer is no. James 4:3 says, "You ask and do not receive, because you ask amiss, that you may spend it on your pleasures." James asserts that when we pray for selfish gain, God responds with no. At other times, it is necessary to wait for God to answer. Perhaps God makes us wait to test our faith and see if we will trust God. Perhaps God in his wisdom is delaying a response until the most opportune moment. On other occasions, God may delay a response to our prayers in order to make us more mature disciples, teaching us trust and self-control.

We cannot develop a strong prayer relationship with God overnight. But we can develop such a relationship if we approach prayer with the right attitude and are willing to give it the time and energy it requires. Aristotle said, "Wishing to be friends is quick work, but friendship is a slow-ripening fruit." So is prayer. But what could be better than developing a relationship with a Father who loves us perfectly and wants to know us intimately and grow us into the people he created us to be? I cannot think of anything that compares with that. And the way to live into that purpose is through prayer.

Appendix A includes a detailed curriculum for a school of prayer that we have developed at Bell's Chapel Church of God. The intent is to teach constituents to pray in keeping with the insights and principles discussed in this chapter. This course was specifically developed to help the congregation cope with the challenges created by the fire at our building. But I am confident that these methods may be used by other congregations dealing with any sort of challenge, even the challenge of daily living.

CHAPTER THREE

PASTORAL CARE AS NARRATIVE THEOLOGY

Narrative literature is one of the main genres in the Bible. More than one-third of Old Testament biblical literature is in the form of extended narrative. Even didactic, poetic, and prophetic genres employ narrative extensively. "Thus says the LORD: 'Keep justice, and do righteousness, for My salvation is about to come, and My righteousness to revealed'" (Isa 56:1).

Approximately half of the New Testament is narrative. Even so, the significance of narrative in the New Testament cannot be assessed simply by the volume of narrative material. The canonical order of books in the New Testament provides a narrative framework to the New Testament as a whole. One might say that the Bible as a whole is organized as a meta-narrative.

Systematic theology has traditionally been an intellectual activity based on thematic, rational analysis and quasi-scientific methodology. One obvious problem that emerges in a discussion of the use of narrative in theology is that narrative seems to have a wholly different structure and logic compared to traditional forms of systematic theology. A narrative may be used to explain something, but it is a different sort of explanation than theology usually offers.

How do systematic theology and narrative theology differ? One might argue that these divergent ways of doing theology vary in assumptions, methodology, and desired outcomes.

In the case of systematic theology, the assumption is that the Scriptures can be approached objectively, relying on logical argument and detailed analysis of the evidence of language, historical data, and other data mined by historical-critical analysis. In other words, systematic theology involves linear progression of thought, argument based on evidence, and abstract ideas.

By contrast, narrative theology assumes the subjective nature of Scripture. The Scriptures are stories about subjects, God, and people that involve concrete details, real-life experiences, and relationships. To do narrative theology, one must rely on elements of story, plot, character, pace, and point of view.

Millard Erickson reflects on the relative value of systematic theology and narrative theology in building Christian faith. He notes that stories communicate "profound truth with dynamic effect." On the other hand, systematic theology is useful in building sound doctrine because of the precise nature of the enterprise. Erickson underlines the difference between theological reflection and the communication of doctrinal content. When comparing systematic and narrative theological method, Erickson urges the church to take a "both-and" rather than an "either-or" approach.[1]

The use of narrative in theology, both to understand and to order theological thought, is of recent interest. And yet narration is a persistent modality across the centuries as faith communities seek to understand Christian redemption. Deriving its incentive from the various influences of theories of literary criticism, social science's interest in personal and biological histories, and philosophical attention to the influence of tradition and character, narrative has become a common topic within Christian theology. This is also in keeping with the keen interest in postmodern worldview with narrative as a way of understanding and making meaning.

---

1. Erickson, *Christian Theology*, 1246.

Michael Goldberg suggests the central place of narration in doing theology: "Narrative or story is a means of expression uniquely suited to theology. Narrative is a perennial category for understanding better how the grammar of religious convictions is displayed and how the self is formed by those convictions."[2]

The majority of Scripture, particularly the Gospels, utilizes narrative form to communicate not only the facts of God's character and work in the world but also the meaning of these facts. The Old Testament tells the story of how God loves his people and of their constant rejection of God. Though the people reject God and worship idols, God is constantly seeking his people to love God and God only. The New Testament employs story form to recount the birth, life, death, and resurrection of our Lord and Savior Jesus Christ.

The Bible is one great book of stories told by the prophets and apostles. But when one looks at the Bible and looks at narrative theology at its most basic, narrative theology is someone else telling God's story. This is even true of the New Testament. Nowhere in the New Testament do we have Jesus writing or telling his story. There is no, "Did I ever tell you about the time I…?" The entire story of Jesus is a third-person narration told by Matthew, Mark, Luke, and John as each presents a certain perspective of the story and events in Jesus' life.

Walter Ewell points to narrative theology as a reclamation project in which scholars recognize the integral character of storytelling to the gospel. In contrast to historical-critical approaches, Ewell suggests that narrative cannot be limited to one feature of the gospel.

Characteristically, theologians employing narrative charge that modern theology sought a prescriptive, organizing

---

2. Goldberg, *Theology and Narrative*, 11.

principle, theme, or system on the basis of which the biblical text was to be understood, usually isolated from the actual shape of Scripture as narrative. Instead of narrative simply being the means to what is truly important behind or beyond the text, narrative theologians argue that it is important precisely because narrative is the revelation of God's identity, particularly in Jesus Christ, and in a corresponding fashion for some, in the life of the church as God's people. Thus, knowledge of God and our identity are available through some form of narrative.[3]

When we look at our lives, or review our lives if we were to tell about us, it would be narrative, a story.

Narrative is embedded in the African-American culture. During the years of slavery much of the spare time of slaves was spent in telling stories of their native land and their hope of a promised land. Messages of freedom events were revealed in story form. Even their stories concerning religion reflect the passion, feeling, and expressiveness of African-American Christianity in a narrative sense.

African-American Christians have, throughout their history, brought to the Bible *a priori* interpretive principles through which the meaning of the Bible was validated. Peter J. Paris observes, "Whenever Scripture is interpreted from the perspective of some tradition other than the black Christian tradition, it fails to speak meaningfully to black people. In fact, it is experienced as alien, irrelevant, insignificant and false. Thus the interpretive framework is more basic than the Scriptures themselves because it alone guarantees meaning."[4]

---

3. Elwell, *Evangelical Dictionary of Theology*, 813.
4. Evans, *We Have Been Believers*, 52.

Hauerwas and Jones offer an analysis of narrative functions in communicating truth. They suggest:

> The category of narrative has been used, among other purposes, to explain human action, to articulate the structures of human consciousness, to depict the identity of agents (whether human or divine), to explain strategies of reading (whether specifically for biblical texts or as a more general hermeneutic), to justify a view of the importance of "storytelling" (often in religious studies through the language of "fables" and "myths"), to account for the historical development of traditions, to provide an alternative to the foundationalist and/or other scientific epistemologies, and to develop a means for imposing order on what is otherwise chaos.[5]

By employing a narrative, one is able to take an abstract principle that is complicated to understand and put it in a form that is relevant and understandable—a story.

How does a storyteller make meaning? Part of the answer to that question lies in understanding the dynamics of the storytelling process. This means thinking about story in a more careful and intentional way by, taking the story apart and assessing how it was assembled from the raw materials available to the storyteller. As one begins such an analysis, the first thing that stands out, is that stories are not merely factual accounts of "what happened." Rather they are carefully crafted *art forms* in which the storyteller selects both what is said (content) and how it is said (form) in a bid to maintain the focus of the reader and to manipulate the response of the audience. From the start, it is critical to note

---

5. Hauerwas and Jones, *Why Narrative?*, 2.

that a story can be told in more than one way. And the way in which a story is told betrays an agenda.[6]

The person conveying the narrative has an outlined plan where he or she is taking the reader. Throughout the storyline the narrative maps out its destination.

George Stroup reflects on the efficacy of narrative theology in explaining the content of belief. His basic question is: Does narrative theology deal precisely enough with the details of theology to be a sufficient method for building doctrinal faith? As an example, he asks, "How is God Creator?" In Stroup's analysis, systematic theology would respond to this query with logical analysis of God's creative activity. A narrative theologian would direct one to read the creation story found in Genesis 1:2–3. In a sense, the two responses represent competing worldviews. A logical, systematic rationale of creation theology is a response based on a modern worldview. Narrative theology is both premodern and postmodern with a priority on storytelling and experience.[7]

The Bible makes no claim that the creation story is a first-person account narrated by God. Rather, it is the narrative of Moses speaking in story form about God, for God. Moses writes, "In the beginning God created the heavens and the earth. The earth was without form, and void; and darkness was on the face of the deep. And the Spirit of God was hovering over the face of the waters. Then God said, 'Let there be light'; and there was light. And God saw the light, that it was good; and God divided the light from the darkness" (Genesis 1:1–4). This is narration at its best. It is Moses telling what God did at the beginning of creation. This is God's creation, this is God's story, but God is not telling the story; another tells it. It is narrative theology, someone else telling God's story.

---

6. Beck, *God as Storyteller*, 4.
7. Stroup, *Promise of Narrative Theology*, 84.

At a more profound level, the origin of the biblical narrative is attributed to the Holy Spirit. Paul asserts, "All Scripture is given by inspiration of God" (2 Tim 3:16). Here Paul claims that the Scriptures represent a divine-human partnership in which God speaks God's story through the Spirit to another, in this case Moses, who resonates with the story and then puts it into words that embody God's word. That's deep! This is the explanation for the authenticity of the Bible. "No prophecy of Scripture is of any private interpretation, for prophecy never came by the will of man, but holy men of God spoke as they were moved by the Holy Spirit" (2 Peter 1:20–21). If the Holy Spirit moved them to speak, it also moved them to narrate, to write another's story.

The Bible rarely claims "Great is the LORD!" without an accompanying story (see Deut 11:7). Stories of God's greatness abound throughout the Bible: God's greatness in giving Sarah a child beyond her childbearing years; God's greatness shown at the Red Sea; God's greatness in feeding the children of Israel in the wilderness with manna from heaven; God's greatness in the battle of Ai when the sun stood still; God's greatness in confusing the enemy for King Jehoshaphat; God's greatness especially made known in Psalm 139. In all of these stories, the biblical authors are retelling a story first placed in their minds and on their hearts by the Holy Spirit.

Ironically, theologians disagree widely on the legitimacy of narrative theology as a hermeneutical pathway of interpretation. Stroup comments:

> Because the use of narrative in theology is a relatively recent development, most theologians have reserved judgment as to whether "narrative theology" is only yet another in a series of fads that have emerged in theological discussion in the 1960s and 1970s, or whether the category has real significance for the interpretation and reconstruction

of Christian doctrine. By no means is it the case that everyone agrees that "narrative" or "story" should become a major motif in systematic theology. Too many issues have yet to be resolved before a convincing argument could be advanced that narrative should play that role. One of the most important of these is the question of the relation between narrative and theology.[8]

What an ironic claim Stroup has made. In fact, narrative theology predates systematic theology by many centuries. One could reasonably make the claim that the use of narrative theology is not so much an innovation as a return to the more original way of working out faith in community. Although it may not have been coined "narrative theology," telling the story of God's redemptive work in the world is the basic fabric of Scripture.

Further, Stroup points to the tendency in the teaching and preaching ministry of the church to use stories as illustrations or motivational devices, what he characterizes as "the mere homiletical or ideological icing on our convictional cake." He seems to be suggesting that modern theology has prized a rational, discursive method while minimizing the importance of narrative. In these comments Stroup raises questions about the substantive quality of narrative theology. Do people tell stories simply for the enjoyment of them, or do stories offer a solid substance of truth that is actually lost in the reductionist practice of analytical theology?[9]

Doing theology requires a context of story to make preaching and teaching effective. For example in the story of Hosea and Gomer, in the book of Hosea, Hosea is told to marry a harlot named Gomer. Gomer is unfaithful to Hosea, leaves Hosea, and is subsequently sold into slavery. This serves as a

8. Ibid., 84.
9. Ibid., 87.

prophetic sign in a story of real people. Without telling this whole story one would miss the fact that God is comparing Hosea and Gomer to the relationship between God's self and Israel. God tells Hosea to go and buy back Gomer to symbolize God's tenacious, resilient love for Israel, who had betrayed him in favor of idolatry. The whole of this narrative must be told in order for the teaching to be effective.

Goldberg offers a detailed argument about the essential nature of narrative in communicating a principle or truth.

> There are many ways of describing narrative; generally speaking, we might say that a narrative is the telling of a story whose meaning unfolds through the interplay of character and actions overtime. Therefore, drawing each of these elements into a single statement, we can now declare that the primary claim of a 'narrative theologian' is that in order to elucidate, examine and transform those deeply held religious beliefs that make a community what it is, one must necessarily show regard for and give heed to those linguistic structures which, through their portrayal of the contingent interaction between persons and events, constitute the source and ground of such beliefs. In short, the fundamental contention is that an adequate theology must attend to narrative.[10]

In other words, Goldberg asserts that the facts of the salvation story are necessary but not sufficient to understanding the story. One must participate in the story to have a sweep of the dynamics: interpersonal interactions, feelings, dramatic events, and the surprising turns of plot. To limit theology to systematic analysis of atonement theory can never capture the drama and reality of the cross.

---

10. Goldberg, *Theology and Narrative*, 35.

Goldberg suggests that narrative approaches to theology might be characterized as post-liberal, philosophical, biblical/literary, and evangelical. He offers a typology of narrative theology in which these approaches can be distinguished, but with the caveat that these methods are not mutually exclusive. More precisely, Goldberg suggests that narrative may be employed in a multiplicity of ways in doing theology. His four categories of narrative include:

- *A post-liberal approach.* Post-liberal concern for narrative stems from the confession that the interpretive center of the Bible is the narration of Jesus' identity, and in turn this narration serves as the basis for early humanity.
- *A philosophical/ethical methodology.* Philosophical and ethical interest in narrative represents a socio-historical understanding of human identity. For H. Richard Niebuhr, God's revelation illumines "the story of our life" in terms of Scripture's story; for Stephen Crites there is a narrative quality of experience; and Paul Ricoeur develops a general theory of narrative interpretation in which a narrativist phenomenology gives rise to human consciousness and understanding.
- *A biblical/literary modality.* Within literary criticism (narrative criticism), biblical scholarship (including interest in narrative theory, the Bible as literature, or canonical forms of criticism), and in theories of biblical narratology or poetics (how meaning is made or explained by putting it into a plot). Narrative captures the story, but the narrative is not the same as the story, exhaustive of the story, or meant to replace the story, yet the story is not given apart from its telling in narrative. There is really no difference in narrative and story, for you cannot give narrative apart from telling the story.

- *An evangelical/doctrinal approach.* Evangelicals have embraced narrative for theology in a variety of ways (literary, theological, and ethical) but most commonly to account for narrational focus of Scripture in relation to questions of truth and history and thus to form a doctrine of Scripture. Accounting for the prominence of narrative is necessary in order to relate historical and theological interests or to account for the identity of God's people.[11]

At a more complex level, narrative theology is a human response to God's revelation of himself. "We begin, not with an inquiry into the possibility of knowing God in principle, but with the conviction that we have been told something we could not tell ourselves," contends John Barton. "And what we have been told has the shape and character of a narrative."[12] Narrative theology, then, might be considered as an investigation into the events about which Scripture tells. This telling about events occurs in the Scriptures, more often than not, through the storytelling process. It is through the act of exploring these stories that one engages in narrative theology and thus a theology of the Scriptures.

Often, legitimate practices of the church are confused with aberrations. Imaginative and faithful storytelling becomes confused with fantasy or flight of thought. Concerns of this nature have haunted narrative theology, as Beck comments:

Narrative theology has become problematic at times when it has been used irresponsibly. When interpreters are unconcerned with the Bible's original meaning and are driven

---

11. Ibid., 36.
12. Barton, "Disclosing Human Possibilities," 54.

by their own intuitions, and even by their own responses to the literature, they often use narrative in harmful ways. The Bible contains huge portions of narrative that are intended to convey truth to us, so it is important for us to adopt some form of narrative theology. Of the sixty-six books in the Bible, twenty-two use story as the primary genre of communication. That is fully one-third of the books in God's inspired Word. Those twenty-two books, whose primary means of communication is the story, account for nearly half the pages in our Bible. So when God has pulled back the curtain of heaven to speak with those of us who live on this side of that veil, God has spoken in story form more often than in any other way. If we believe that a divine voice lies behind the pages of our Bible, then we must acknowledge that the God who speaks there is a storyteller.[13]

That Scripture is narrative is demonstrated in the gospel of Luke. "Then He said to them, 'O foolish ones, and slow of heart to believe in all that the prophets have spoken! Ought not the Christ to have suffered these things and to enter into His glory?' And beginning at Moses and all the Prophets, He expounded to them in all the Scriptures the things concerning Himself" (Luke 24:25–27). Here Luke informs the reader of the larger story of Jesus found in the Old Testament prophets who gave a narrative about him and his suffering on our behalf.

Hans Frei challenges theologians to go beyond surface categories of narrative and to ask how the gospel story is an experience of the incarnation. "The Word became flesh and dwelt among us" (John 1:14). He rejects the assumption that the narrative quality of the Bible begins with the human penchant for story. Rather, Frei emphasizes the way in which biblical narrative fleshes out God's covenant with humanity. The nexus

---

13. Beck, *God as Storyteller*, 1.

of the biblical story is the life, death, and resurrection of Jesus Christ.[14]

Drawing on a neo-orthodox perspective of revelation, Loughlin underlines the distinctive quality of the biblical narrative as a story like no other. His claim of uniqueness of the biblical narrative relies upon the revelatory nature of the story. This is not a story that people made up or discovered. The biblical narrative is a God-given and God-authored story through its writers. As such, the biblical narrative does not need to fit the story line of the world or operate in keeping with a secular worldview. In a sense, the strange, alien character of the biblical narrative is a testimony to its authenticity. After all, these stories had different origins and different authorship from any other stories. He concludes his argument by suggesting that narrative theology can be a powerful form of apologetics, an alternative to point-by-point reasoning about the truth of the gospel. In narrative theology, one proclaims a true story about the one who is the Way and the Truth and the Life.[15]

Rightly used, narrative theology provides the building blocks for systematic and for biblical theology. One might say that systematic theology tends to default to building theology from more propositional literature (e.g., the New Testament letters). On the other hand, Old Testament biblical theology tends to depend primarily on narrative for its theological building blocks.

Stephen Kepnes reflects on the way narrative theology connects faith issues in the ancient context with faith issues in the twentieth century. He asks, "How can the Bible, a text from a radically different era, address our situation today?" His argument is that the Bible operates with both a concrete groundedness in a given time and place and a sense of God's timeless

---

14. Frei, *Theology and Narrative*, 208.
15. Loughlin, *Telling God's Story*, 36.

relationship to the world. As such, the biblical narrative takes seriously the concrete details of this century because it asserts that God takes seriously the concrete circumstances of God's people. Kepnes cites Martin Buber's observation that concrete events are the substance of the biblical narrative: "Events, unplanned, unexpected events which transformed the historical situation of the community, lie at the root of the biblical narratives and biblical faith."[16]

Theologians use the term *myth* to point to the relationship of the biblical narratives to systematic theology. Theological propositions rely on timeless stories, that is, myths of faith. According to Terrene Tilley, one of the narrative forms employed by the Scripture is *myth*. "A story is a myth," Tilley explains, "if it 'sets up' a world for people to dwell in or constitutes a tradition for people to live in."[17] Understood in this way, then, *myth* is a neutral term. It does not necessarily denote a literally untrue account or fantasy of events. Yet even fictional stories can be "profoundly true, rich in powerfully persuasive meanings."[18]

But what about the biblical tradition of historical revelation? Is it too mythological, or does it (as many adherents have claimed) lie entirely outside myth as a historical and "factual" disclosure of God's nature and will?

If by historical revelation one means the disclosure of God in and through real historical events, then the argument could be made that mythology is a legitimate means of attaching meaning to conventional history. By mythology one does not mean lies or falsehoods, but rather the narrative disclosure of ultimate meaning for our lives through historical events.

---

16. Kepnes, *Text as Thou*, 125.
17. Tilley, *Story Theology*, 40.
18. Borg, *Reading the Bible Again*, 62.

Sacred history is not a mere chronicle of events, but an interpreted account of what those events mean within a narrative historical construal or reading of them. In other words, people understand the events of history in the light of a narrative plot which links those events into a meaningful whole.[19]

William Bausch draws upon the metaphor of a tapestry in an attempt to capture the organic way that Scripture is narrative.

Scripture is story; that story, like all art forms, is a free expression of something deeper; and, finally, that story, like all art forms, is highly pluralistic. As in art, there are many diverse, imaginative weaves in story's fabric. In announcing the mystery there must be metaphor, parable, poetry, legend, and all the rest, with more than one way to tell it. Which is why we really do not have a doctrine, say, of creation. We have stories of creation.[20]

The incarnate Word is a story-word in which God dwells. Bausch underlines the way in which biblical stories make relationships with God come alive for contemporary readers by recounting God's history of relationships. He asserts that God is known not by discovery of facts about God but by experiencing God as a person. Some of this experience of God is direct. But much of one's experience of God is by observation of other faithful people as they work out the details of a relationship with God in the circumstances of life. The Bible is full of such accounts of faith under fire that serve to guide, sustain, and inspire people in every age. To read the stories of God's people

---

19. Brockelman, *Inside Story*, 103.
20. Bausch, *Storytelling*, 110.

in the Bible is to have an intimate connection with them and with God.[21]

The use of narrative in theology tends to blur a number of methodological distinctions in modern theology. For example, systematic theology operates by strict principles of division among historical, literary, and theological approaches. Narrative is a holistic approach that draws upon all of these resources. Likewise, narrative theology does not engage in dualistic constructs of story and fiction, history and truth. Narrative theology concentrates on how the text is received and used within Christian faith, sometimes deferring questions of historical reference, which causes discomfort among some evangelicals. The study of narrative reminds us that biblical scholars are practitioners of theology, and theologians are also interpreters of biblical narrative. In many ways the argument between more narrative approaches and more discursive approaches to theology seems to be a debate about precision and the importance of certain details.

> One of the important ways in which God's story gets told is in the telling from one generation to the next. Each generation of believers finds itself compelled to reinterpret and retell the story of God for itself and its contemporaries, and yet each generation also depends profoundly upon its inheritance from those who have gone before in the faith. For it is not enough simply to hand the Bible over to our children; rather, we will tell and live and grapple with God's Story anew in every age, and also bequeath to our successors the same process of telling and living and grappling.[22]

Moses encourages the children of Israel to use narratives regarding their experiences with God.

---

21. Beck, *God as Storyteller*, 36.
22. Lodahl, *Story of God*, 25.

Hear, O Israel: The LORD our God, the LORD is one! You shall love the LORD your God with all your heart, with all your soul, and with all your strength. And these words which I command you today shall be in your heart. You shall teach them diligently to your children, and shall talk of them when you sit in your house, when you walk by the way, when you lie down, and when you rise up. You shall bind them as a sign on your hand, and they shall be as frontlets between your eyes. You shall write them on the doorposts of your house and on your gates. (Deut 6:4–9)

This was Moses' way of narrative theology. Proponents of narrative theology suggest that the use of stories as an organic way of teaching and building faith continues to be a primary way of faithful communities.

Bell's Chapel Church of God has a story of the struggles endured after fire destroyed our place of worship, mission, and outreach. As pastor, I find myself telling and retelling this story of the congregation's struggles—the defeats and the victories. As the story is told, the faith community continues to learn about God's faithfulness at a deeper level. The faith story of Bell's Chapel can be a witness to the world at large that God is still at work in human lives, and it becomes the context of our prayer ministry. As we face new challenges to our faith and call upon God for help, we recall his redemptive work in our past and praise him for making us the church we are today.

This chapter has examined the contours of narrative theology as it supports a ministry of prayer and the practice of pastoral care through the Word of God for every situation. This experience has strengthened my faith in God and God's Word. It has had a powerful impact on my own prayer life. In many ways, the process of writing and reflection has sharpened my ministry of pastoral care and my ability to engage in ministries of healing, guiding, sustaining, and reconciliation with the members of my congregation.

Reflecting on our experience has helped me make sense of a blur of events. Looking back, I can see the progression of God's blessings on the life of the church. Stories of grief, conflict, and anxiety help me understand the struggle of our faith community with greater compassion and insight. God's grace has been at work preparing the way, sustaining us, guiding us, and strengthening us. God does not always take us in the direction we want to go to get the results we want, yet we can trust God's leading into the perfection of his will.

A TRAINING COURSE IN PRAYER

I. Desired Outcomes

Prayer is a spiritual experience that involves human activity but it is not limited to human activity. As such, the evaluation of training in prayer and desired outcomes is more qualitative than quantitative. From a research perspective, the training program might be evaluated in terms of cognitive, affective, and behavioral shifts in participants. Drawing on these categories of human functioning, some desired outcomes of the training program are:

1. The participants will demonstrate increased understanding of the nature of prayer, forms of prayer, and a theology of prayer.
2. The participants will deepen appreciation for the part prayer plays in their lives as demonstrated by testimonies of spiritual experiences through prayer.
3. The participants will demonstrate increased understanding of the relationship between prayer and attitudes.
4. The participants will spend more time in communion with God in prayer both in daily practice and in faithfulness to prayer over an extended period of time.
5. The participants will deepen their understanding of community dimensions of prayer.

2. A Course Outline

Week One: THE ESSENCE OF PRAYER
Begin class with prayer and discuss that prayer is simply talking to God. End class by allowing participants to practice praying.
Bible focus: Luke 11:1–13

Week Two: PRAYER BEGINS WITH PRAISE
Begin class with praise songs. Discuss praise words, e.g. *Hallelujah*, *Praise the Lord*, etc.
Discuss "Hallowed be thy name."

Week Three: PRAYING ALOUD
Discuss James 1:5–7, Isaiah 59:1–8
Practice praying aloud.

Week Four: WHAT SHOULD WE PRAY ABOUT?
Bible focus: Philippians 4:6–7
Have participants make a list of prayer concerns.

3. Feedback Questionnaire

Thank you for taking a moment to give your feedback on ways that you learned to pray during our four weekly sessions. We want to continue the great work that God has begun in your prayer life, and we want your feedback. Please rate these responses on a scale of 1–5. 1=Not at all, and 5=Very much. Please give your survey to your pastor or turn it in at the office.

1. I have developed a greater desire to pray.
   1 2 3 4 5

2. I am spending more time in prayer on a daily basis.
   1 2 3 4 5

3. Since I changed my prayer habits, I feel closer to God through prayer.
   1 2 3 4 5

4. I have learned to pray in new ways that I really value.
   1 2 3 4 5

5. The class helped me grow in my prayer life and relationship to God.
   1 2 3 4 5

6. I would like to have more classes on this subject.
   1 2 3 4 5

7. I would recommend this class to others.
   1 2 3 4 5

Please tell a story or share a testimony about ways God has worked in your life or the lives of others through prayer since you have taken this class.

APPENDIX B

NARRATIVE SERMONS ON PRAYER

"Keep On Pushing"
2 Chronicles 7:14–15; Luke 18:1–8

At times in our lives, and especially on this Christian journey, it seems as if we want to give up and throw in the towel. Sometimes when we try to do our best, new temptations, new trials, or something else pulls us off course. No matter what we try to do, sometimes it seems we can never get it right. Just as Paul says, when we would do right, evil is always present. We might even try to pray and end up saying to ourselves, and to God, "What's the use?" So we give up and stop praying. But I came to encourage you today to hold on and to hold out because your blessing is just around the corner. You have to keep on looking up, keep on trusting, and keep on pushing until your change comes.

You see, Job, in all of his loses, in all of his afflictions, during all of his troubles, never gave up. There were times when he got discouraged and said, "All of my appointed time, I'm going to wait until my change comes." Job kept on pushing. Anybody going to wait until your change comes today?

Even Jesus, when it came to dying on the cross, got discouraged and didn't want to die. But he said to God in the end, "Not my will but Thine be done." And Jesus kept on pushing. So today, brothers and sisters in Christ, I want you to know that Jesus doesn't want us to be weary in well-doing and doesn't want us to give up, for the Bible says that we shall reap if we faint not.

Then Isaiah 40:30–31 reminds us that "even the youths shall faint and grow weary, And the young men shall utterly fall, But those who wait on the LORD shall renew their strength; They shall mount up with wings like eagles, They shall run and not be weary, They shall walk and not faint." So today by the power of the Holy Spirit I want to encourage you to wait on the Lord, to hold on, to not give up, and to keep on pushing for your breakthrough. Your blessing is on the way. Will you pray with me as I preach/teach on the subject, "Keep on Pushing"?

I'm pressing on the upward way,
New heights I'm gaining every day;
Still praying as I'm onward bound,
"Lord, plant my feet on higher ground."
My heart has no desire to stay
Where doubts arise and fears dismay;
Though some may dwell where these abound,
My prayer, my aim, is higher ground.
Lord, lift me up and let me stand
By faith on Canaan's tableland;
A higher plane than I have found,
Lord, plant my feet on higher ground.[1]

Anybody want to go higher in the Lord today?

Our Scripture lesson text today is taken from the gospel according to Luke. Luke, not a disciple of Jesus Christ, writes his gospel from his association with Paul and from his research. Luke says to Theophilus, a governor or perhaps just a close friend, in the first chapter that he surfed the Internet, Googled

---

1. "Higher Ground." Lyrics by Johnson Oatman. Public domain.

the name *Jesus*, read his *Encyclopedia Britannica*, texted the disciples, and checked the library about this man Jesus, so what he writes in his gospel is accurate and oh so true.

Luke, known as the beloved physician, writes the longest and most comprehensive of the four Gospels. Luke, presenting Jesus as the Son of Man who came to seek and save the lost, introduces Jesus as a babe born to a virgin, wrapped in swaddling clothes and laid in a manger, who at his birth had the Golden Globe Angel Singers, hailing "Glory to God in the highest and on earth peace and goodwill toward men."

The news of Jesus' birth went around the world faster than the news that a black man just became president of the United States; for shepherds who were in the field keeping watch over their flocks by night, without the aid of CNN news or the *Amos Brown Show*, heard that a Savior was born who is Christ the Lord, and he shall save his people from their sins.

For the word went out, the gossip was hot, saying, "Unto us a Child is born, Unto us a Son is given; And the government shall be upon his shoulder. And his name will be called Wonderful," for he's better than Wonder Bread. His name shall be called Counselor, for you can tell him the deepest secret of your heart and he won't tell a soul. His name shall be called the Everlasting Father, for his kingdom shall be from everlasting to everlasting. His name shall be called the Prince of Peace, for in him is real peace, a peace that the world cannot give, a peace that you can't find in marijuana or Long Island ice teas, and it is a peace that the world cannot take away. For when everything is going wrong in your life, Jesus can give you that peace, that like a river "attendeth your way…when sorrows like seas billows roll. Whatever your lot," if you have the Prince of Peace in your life, you'll be able to say it is well, it is well with your soul. Anybody got that Jesus peace today?

Luke in his gospel takes us from the birth to the cross, from the cross to the grave, from the grave to the sky as Jesus leaves the disciples singing, "Praise him, praise him, praise him, praise him, Jesus blessed Savior." And he is worthy to be praised. Amen?

Our text today takes place in chapter eighteen of the gospel according to Luke and talks about a woman, with an adversary, who sought justice from an unjust judge and would not give up but kept on pushing. There are several things I want to bring to your attention in this message, and then I'll be finished.

The first thing is that prayer is very important in our Christian lives. And no matter how slow it seems that God is in hearing and answering our prayers, we should keep on praying until something happens. These verses in this text teach us, first, the great importance of perseverance in prayer. Notice in the text that this woman's prayer wasn't answered because she got an attitude with God, nor because she gave up; her prayer was answered because she was persistent in praying.

Verse 1 reads, "Then He [Jesus] spoke a parable to them, that men always ought to pray and not lose heart." Jesus is saying that no matter what the problem is, what the situation may be, that we should tell him all about our troubles, and he will hear our faintest cry and answer by and by. Prayer should always interest Christians. Prayer is the very life-breath of true Christianity.

When Jesus says that we ought to always pray and not lose heart, this does not mean that a person should be constantly performing the act of prayer. It means that a person should constantly keep up the habit of prayer and endeavor to be always in a prayerful frame of mind. And if you want to be close to the Lord, then we should always pray; for Psalm 145:18 reads, "The LORD is near to all who call upon Him, To all who call upon Him in truth. He will fulfill the desire of those who fear Him; He also will hear their cry and save them." So we should always have a prayerful frame of mind and talk to God about everything and anything that bothers us; for 1 Peter 5:7 says to cast "all [our] care upon Him, for He cares for [us]."

If you notice in the text, it says that this woman wanted to get justice from her adversary. We don't know if someone had taken her child because of some debt that she owed, if someone had taken some property from her, if someone held her dowry, or what the problem was. What we do know is that she went to the judge and the judge would not hear her, so she kept going, she kept going, and she kept going to the judge to hear her cry.

Brothers and sisters in Christ, sometimes God will not answer our prayers right at first. Sometimes God wants to see if we really mean what we are asking for in prayer and if we have the faith that he can do what we are asking. Matthew 7:7–8 says, "Ask, and it will be given to you; seek, and you will find; knock, and it will be opened to you. For everyone who asks receives, and he who seeks finds, and to him who knocks it will be opened." Even though this passage says to ask, seek, and knock it means to keep asking, keep seeking, and keep knocking. Sometimes we just can't go to God and ask one time and the world gets turned upside down. Sometimes we have to labor in prayer for God to hear and answer our prayer. But don't give up. That's why the first thing Jesus said in this chapter was, "Men always ought to pray and not lose heart."

There will be times when we will call on God and think that we need him right that second, and sometimes he will show up right that second. But, oh, if you have to wait on him, wait on him and be of good courage, for he may not come when you want him, but he's always on time because he's an on time God, yes he is.

The next thing I want to bring to your attention in this message is that sometimes we have to check our status quo with God to see if we are in good standing for him to hear and answer our prayer. Second Chronicles 7:14-15 reads, "If My people who are called by My name will humble themselves, and pray and seek My face, and turn from their wicked ways, then I will hear from heaven, and will forgive their sin and heal their land. Now My eyes will be open and My ears attentive to prayer made in this place."

The first thing I want to notice in this passage is that it says, "Who are called by My name." Brothers and sisters in Christ, God will not hear your prayer if you have not given your life to him. God does not hear sinners' prayers. The only prayer of a sinner that God will hear is "Lord save me."

Then too, we have to make sure that we are in right standing with God for him to hear us. The next thing the passage says, "...will humble themselves, and pray and seek My face, and turn from their wicked ways." God does not want to hear our prideful call to him. God does care about where you work, how much you have in your 401(k), where you live, what you drive, or how much money you have, because when it comes down to it, it all belongs to him. But God wants us to humble ourselves before him, and seek his will for our lives, and turn from the sinful lives that we are living. He says, "Then I will hear from heaven." Some of our attitudes toward God have to change before he will do anything about our situations.

This week I had an electrician here at the church to work on the light for our new sign out front. He came and started working on the light; then he called me and said, "Bishop, there is a problem between the sign and the junction box, and I have to go underground to see if I can make a direct connection to the box to get power to the sign." He went on to say that somewhere there was a loose connection and some weakness between the box and the sign. You see, in order for the sign to work properly the right connection had to be made from the box to the sign.

Some of you know where I am headed with this. In order for God to hear and answer our prayer, we have to have the right connection between our lives and Him. Some of our prayers God is not hearing nor answering because there is a problem between us and Him. Some of us harbor iniquity in our hearts, and the Bible says if I regard iniquity (sin) in my heart, the Lord will not hear me.

Some of our prayers are not being answered because we have not forgiven someone, and the Bible says, "Forgive us our debts as we forgive our debtors." Some of us are not forgiving someone in our lives who has done something to us, so since we will not forgive them, neither is God forgiving us.

If you have unresolved domestic problems, that too can keep God from hearing and answering your prayer. First Peter 3:7 reads, "Husbands, likewise, dwell with them with understanding, giving honor to the wife, as to the weaker vessel, and as being heirs together of the grace of life, that your prayers may not be hindered." You cannot have something between you and your spouse if you want your prayers to be answered. God says the same in 2 Chronicles—we have to turn from our wicked ways if we want God to hear us.

The next thing I want to bring to your attention in this message is that if this judge had mercy on this widow, how do you think God will feel about us if we keep asking him? In the text it says that this judge did not fear God nor regard man, but because this woman kept on pushing he gave her what she asked him for. You see, my dear people, the God we serve is a counterexample to the judge in our text today. The judge in the text was not compassionate; he didn't care anything about mankind. But the Bible says in Lamentations 3:22 that the God we serve is compassionate: Because of the Lord's great love "we are not consumed, because His compassions fail not." So God is opposite of this judge in that the God we serve is compassionate. The judge in our text was not good, but we know that the God we serve—our judge—is a good God. He's a great God and can do anything but fail.

Psalm 118:1 reads, "Oh, give thanks to the LORD, for He is good! For His mercy endures forever." And many of us in this room today can testify to the fact that God is good. For when our enemy could have overtaken us, the good God we serve stepped in and moved our enemy out of the way. When Satan could have sifted us as wheat, the good God we serve told Satan to back up, give him fifty feet, and the good God allowed us to stomp on the Devil's head. When our bills were due and the baby needed shoes, the good God we serve sent a check in the mail. God is good, amen?

The judge in the text was not a merciful judge, but the God we serve is plenteous in mercy and abounding in grace. Lamentations 3:22–23 reads, "Through the LORD's mercies we are not consumed, Because His compassions fail not. They are new every morning." And I don't know about you, but I thank God for his mercy and that his mercy endures forever. For if it had not been for the Lord, who was on my side with his mercy, I could have been dead and sleeping in my grave. And if it had not been for the Lord, who was on your side, some of those drugs that you took, you could have overdosed, but because of two bad boys named goodness and mercy following you all the days of your life, you are here today. If it had not been for the Lord, who was on your side and those two bad boys named goodness and mercy, that bullet that missed you could have hit you and you could be dead and sleeping in your grave. If it had not been for the Lord, who was on your side, and those two bad boys named goodness and mercy when the police were after you and you got away, you could have been sitting in some cold prison, but because of the mercy of God…So the God we serve is much different from the judge in this text in that God loves us, cares for us, and wants the very best for his children. Somebody tell God thank you!

The last thing I want to bring to your attention is that no matter how long it takes God to answer, you just keep on pushing; for, as James 5:16 says, "the effective, fervent prayer of a righteous man avails much." In the text the woman kept on asking and pleading with this judge to avenge her of her adversary, and it says that since this woman kept worrying him and troubling him, he granted her request. Now listen to what Jesus says in verse 7 of Luke 18: "And shall God not avenge His own elect who cry out day and night to Him, though He bears long with them?" Jesus is saying that if this judge, who is wicked has no regard for God nor for man, can hear and answer this woman's request, then won't God hear you if you keep on calling on his name?

Brothers and sisters in Christ, God does not begrudge answering prayer. Jesus' point is that if an insensitive judge will respond to the continual requests of a widow, God will certainly respond to the continual prayers of a believer.

So today I came to encourage many of you who have given up on praying not to give up but to keep on pushing in prayer. In Scripture there are persons who kept on pushing in prayer, and God heard them and did something about it:

"Come here, Hannah." "Well, I'm glad you asked me here, Bishop Adrienne. I was barren and I wanted a child. I went to the temple and didn't stand and voice my prayer, but I prayed in my heart, just moving my mouth. The priest thought I was drunk, but I was drunk in prayer. I prayed and I prayed, and I prayed. I kept on pushing in prayer and finally God heard me, opened my womb and gave me a man child." God hears and answers prayer but sometimes you have to keep on pushing.

"Come here, old man Hezekiah." "Well, thank you for asking me here today, Bishop Adrienne. One day old man Isaiah came to my house and told me to get ready because I was surely going to die. Well, I didn't want to die, I wasn't ready to die, and so I turned my face to the wall. I whispered a prayer in the morning. I whispered a prayer at noon. I whispered a prayer in the evening. I kept on pushing in prayer, and Isaiah came back to my house and told me I could stop praying because God had heard my prayer and added fifteen more years to my life."

Let me see if I can get two last witnesses. "Come here, Paul and Brother Silas." "Thank you for asking us here today, Bishop Adrienne. We were bound in a cold jail in shackles and chains, and at midnight Silas started singing, 'It's me, it's me, it's me, oh Lord, standing in the need of prayer.' And I, Paul, started praying, 'Come by here, oh Lord, come by here. Somebody needs you Lord; come by here.' We kept pushing in prayer, and the jail house began to rock, our chains fell off, and we walked out of the jail singing. 'Free at last, free at last. Thank God almighty, I'm free at last.'"

We can bring this thing closer to home. One day some of you were involved in some court cases, and you kept on pushing in prayer, and God showed up in the courtroom and worked things out. Somebody tell God thank you.

Some of you were involved in drugs, and you kept on pushing in prayer, and God delivered you from those drugs. Somebody tell God thank you.

Some of you were involved in some bad deals, and you began to pray. Nobody else knew you were praying, but you would go into your secret closet, shut the door, fall on your knees, and say, "I must tell Jesus all of my troubles." You kept on pushing in prayer, and God heard you and delivered you. Brothers and sisters in Christ, it may seem like God is far away, and God is not listening to your cry, but you fall on your knees, ask God for forgiveness, and begin to push your way in prayer, and watch God show up.

"Do You Have What It Takes to Stand?"
Genesis 22:1–18; 1 Peter 4:12–13

Throughout my walk with the Lord my faith has been tested. In 1995 when the Lord spoke to me and told me to quit a job paying over $62,000 a year, my faith was tested. When my children were taken from me and I went to court without a lawyer, knowing that I had done nothing wrong, my faith was tested. June 11, 2000, when I took the church Bell's Chapel Church of God, with just six people, my faith was tested. March 23, 2008, when I planted Abounding Grace Church of God, my faith was tested. Over the last year, with the burning of Bell's Chapel, the finances, and the rebuilding of the church, both my faith and my patience have been tested. But you know what, brothers and sisters in Christ? No matter what test comes my way, I've promised the Lord that I would.

You see, the way that my faith and patience is being tested now, I remember a time when I would say, "Forget it. I'll get in my car and ride, and you'll never see me again." But this time I can't and I won't do that. I can't run, because I am committed to what God has called me to do. I won't run because there are some of you who know what I am going through, who have heard me preach and are watching to see just what I am going to do. And I promise you today I'm not going to let you down because I know without a doubt the Lord will bring us out.

You see, when we face a test, God knows what the outcome of the test will be, but that old devil, Satan himself, tries to get us to turn our backs on God and run. But the Bible tells us not to run but to be steadfast, unmovable, and always abounding in the work of the Lord, knowing that our labor is not in vain. Then when we have tried everything that we can do, after we have put our faith to work, after we have asked, sought, and knocked, the Bible tells us to just stand. Ephesians 6:13–16 reads, "Therefore take up the whole armor of God, that you may be able to withstand in the evil day, and having done all, to stand. Stand therefore, having girded your waist with truth, having put on the breastplate of righteousness, and having shod your feet with the preparation of the gospel of peace."

You see, brothers and sisters in Christ, as soldiers in the army of God we are not commanded to fight, we are just commanded to stand; and when we stand, we aren't standing alone, but we are standing with the Lord on our side. If God be for us, who can be against us? Will you pray with me as I preach/teach on the subject, "Do You Have What It Takes to Stand?"

> *Standing of the promises of Christ my King,*
> *Through eternal ages let His praises ring,*
> *Glory in the highest, I will shout and sing,*
> *Standing on the promises of God.*
> *Standing on the promises that cannot fail,*
> *When the howling storms of doubt and fear assail,*
> *By the living Word of God I shall prevail,*
> *Standing on the promises of God.*
> *Standing, standing,*
> *Standing on the promises of God my Savior;*
> *Standing, standing,*
> *I'm standing on the promises of God.*[2]

Do I have any persons in the room today who are standing on his promises? The promise that even though we don't have all that we want, we know that he will supply all of our needs according to his riches in glory? The promise that even though our friends walk out on us when our money is funny we have the promise that he, Jesus, will never leave us nor forsake us? The promise that when our enemies try to throw darts at us no weapon formed against us shall prosper? The promise that when

---

2. "Standing on the Promises." Lyrics by R. Kelso Carter. Public domain.

our mother and father forsake us then the Lord will take us up? Do I have anybody standing on the promises of God?

Our Scripture lesson text today is taken from the book of Genesis. Genesis is the book of beginnings. Its fifty chapters sketch human history from Creation to the Tower of Babel (chapters 1–11) and from Abraham to Joseph (chapters 12–50). The first eleven chapters introduce the Creator God and the beginnings of life, sin, judgment, family, worship, and salvation. The remainder of the book focuses on the lives of the four patriarchs of the faith: Abraham, Isaac, Jacob, and Joseph, from whom will come the nation of Israel and ultimately the Savior, Jesus Christ. Somebody tell God thank you for Jesus.

The first part of the book of Genesis focuses on the beginning and spread of sin in the world and culminates in the devastating flood in the days of Noah. The second part of the book focuses on God's dealing with one man, Abraham, through whom God promises to bring salvation and blessing to the world in the person of Jesus Christ.

Abraham and his descendants learn firsthand that it is always safe to trust the Lord in times of famine and feasting, blessing and bondage. And just let me encourage you here today that we can always trust God in everything and through everything. Although we may not see him working in our times of struggle, we can rest assured that he is working on our behalf, and he is going to turn around every bad thing and work it out for our good if we just hold on and hold out; for the Bible says in Romans 8:28 that "all things work together for good to those who love God, to those who are called according to His purpose." And the very thing that Satan meant for bad, God is going to work it out for our good. Turn to your neighbor and tell them God is working it out, and he's working it out for your good.

Although Genesis does not directly name its author; and although Genesis ends some three centuries before Moses was born, the whole of Scripture and church history are unified in their adherence to the Mosaic authorship of Genesis, that Moses himself, under the direction and the influence of an almighty God, wrote this book.

The book of Genesis was written to present the beginning of everything except God, because before there was a here or a there, a when or a where, there was God, and without God we could do nothing. Without him how we would fail. Without God our lives would be rugged, like a ship without a sail.

I can't tell you where God came from because God has always been God, but I can tell you what he feels like when he moves. God feels like a clapping in my hands; God feels like a running and jumping in my feet; God feels like a hallelujah in my praise; and God feels like fire shut up in my bones. Anybody else know what God feels like?

Our Scripture lesson text is found in Genesis 22, where a man named Abraham has been called to offer up a special sacrifice to God, his only son, Isaac. And with this request God tests Abraham to see if he has what it takes to stand. There are several things I want to bring to your attention in this message, and then I'll be finished.

The first is that at some point in time in our Christian walk, God will test our faith. Genesis 22:1–3 says, "Now it came to pass after these things that God tested Abraham, and said to him, 'Abraham!' And he said, 'Here I am.' Then He said, 'Take now your son, your only son Isaac, whom you love, and go to the land of Moriah, and offer him there as a burnt offering on one of the mountains of which I shall tell you.' So Abraham rose early in the morning and saddled his donkey, and took two of his young men with him, and Isaac his son; and he split the wood for the burnt offering and arose and went to the place of which God had told him."

Brothers and sisters in Christ, for every test God puts us through, he knows how we will react to the test and whether we will pass or fail even before the test begins, because the God we serve is omniscient, meaning he knows all. Here God tells Abraham to take his only son, God says, the son "whom you love," and offer him as a sacrifice. When God told Abraham to take his son and offer him as a sacrifice—notice not just as a sacrifice but as a burnt sacrifice, meaning kill him and then burn him up—God knew that Abraham was going to do just what he told him to do. God knew how Abraham was going to act and react, but God still put him to the test.

When God puts us to the test, God knows how we are going to react. God knew how Daniel was going to react when he had him thrown into the lion's den. God knew Daniel's reaction was going to be to pray in the midst of the lions.

God knew how Shadrach, Meshach, and Abednego were going to act when they got ready to be thrown into the furnace. God knew that no matter what, these three Hebrew boys were not going to bow down and worship anything but God, no matter how much pressure they were under or what the outcome would be.

God knew how Paul and Silas were going to act when they were thrown into the Roman jail. God knew that Silas was going to sing. And God knew that while Silas was singing Paul was going to be praying, "Father, I stretch my hands to Thee, No other help I know."

When God tests us, God knows what the outcome of the test will be, but he wants to see how we will handle the test while we are going through it. God wants to see if we will pass the test by praying. God wants to see if during our times of testing we will pray without ceasing. God wants to see if we will remember the telephone number to heaven. Jeremiah 33:3 says, "Call to Me, and I will answer you, and show you great and mighty things, which you do not know."

God wants to see if during our times of testing we will know how to stamp our prayer letter to heaven so that our prayers will be answered and we will be able to get a prayer through. You see, in order for God to answer our prayers, every prayer has to end in the name of Jesus; for Jesus tells us that if we ask anything in his name, he will do it. And whatever we ask in his name, Jesus says that the Father, who is God, will do it.

Sometimes during our test it is hard to pray, so we have to learn to pray breath prayers. A breath prayer is one sentence or one word. Sometimes we can only say, "Lord, help." Sometimes we can only say, "Have mercy, Jesus." Sometimes we can only say, "Lord come and see about me." Sometimes we can only say, "I need Thee, oh, I need Thee." But no matter what we say, just keep the prayer line open to heaven and I promise you, you will pass the test.

Then God wants to see if we will pass the test by our praise. You see, as we go through our test, God will exchange some things as we pass each phase of the test. Isaiah 61 says God will "give them beauty for ashes, the oil of joy for mourning, and the garment of praise for the spirit of heaviness." You see, the things that look ugly to us God says he will make to look beautiful during our testing times. That eviction notice, which may be your test, looks ugly to you, but if you praise God, God will cover it with a beautiful check from some place you didn't even expect. That's the beauty for ashes. They may repossess your car and you catch the bus for a while, and that may make you mourn for a while. But you save a little bit of money and that truck you were looking at with the twenty-inch rims will be parked in your driveway next week. And the new truck, that's the oil of joy for mourning.

Now, the garment of praise for the spirit of heaviness is what we will receive when we "enter into His gates with thanksgiving and into His courts with praise" and we begin to bless his name. When we begin to praise our way through, the test doesn't seem so bad and the test doesn't seem so long.

Sometimes we can praise ourselves lighter so that the burden we walked into church with, when we walk out—if we really get our praise on while we are here—seems lighter to carry.

When we clap our hands in praise, we upset the Devil, because where Satan thought he had us, our praise confuses him and he has to try some new schemes and some new tactics. You see, when we praise our way through, as we start shouting, "Hallelujah" and "Thank you, Jesus," Satan gets upset so he flees from us for a while and goes back to see if he can get something else to discourage us and make us give up on God.

But I came to tell you today that if you want to stand during the test, 1 Thessalonians 5:18 says, "In everything give thanks; for this is the will of God in Christ Jesus for you." So for your test, give God some praise. For your storm, give God some praise. For your bad time, give God some praise. For your cloudy skies, give God some praise. For not being able to see your way, give God some praise because when praises go up, blessings come down.

The next thing I want to bring to your attention in this message is that we have to believe—to have faith that God can—before God will. Notice in verse 5 it reads, "And Abraham said to his young men, 'Stay here with the donkey; the lad and I will go yonder and worship, and we will come back to you.'" In the last part of this passage I read to you it said that God told Abraham to offer Isaac as a burnt offering. Now, if you notice, Abraham tells the persons who accompanied him that "we will come back to you." So if Abraham had to offer Isaac as a sacrifice, then how could "we," meaning Abraham and Isaac, come back? Abraham had the faith that, since he trusted God, God could and would do something to save his only son whom he loved. But first, Abraham said, "I have to worship." Abraham knew that he could increase his faith and gain the strength to do what God had commanded him to do from God, and from God alone; but first Abraham had to worship.

Sometimes in order to get our faith to start working, we have to start worshiping. When we start going through our storms and through our test, we can't give up on God and stay at home and not come to worship. Hebrews 10:25 tells us to not forsake "the assembly of ourselves together…but [exhort] one another," meaning come to church, and when you get here testify. So we have to press our way to the house of the Lord and worship God during our times of testing.

We have to have an attitude of gratitude and tell God, even though we are going through, "I was glad when they said to me, 'Let us go into the house of the Lord.'" Then when we get here, we have to tell somebody, "I'm going through, but I'm here, so 'Oh, magnify the Lord with me, And let us exalt His name together" (Ps 34:3).

Sometimes we have to speak over ourselves and encourage our own selves in the Lord. Sometimes when we can't see our way we have to say to ourselves, "Take courage," and we have to believe that the God we serve will make a way.

Brothers and sisters in Christ, when we trust God and when we truly have faith in God, God may allow Satan to make us feel at times as if we are in quicksand, but God—if we just believe that God can—will deliver us from whatever test we are going through. We may feel like we are in quicksand and sinking, but if we know that God can, then God will not allow us to fall, because, as Deuteronomy 33:27 says, "The eternal God is your refuge, and underneath are the everlasting arms." We may feel like we are going under, but underneath us are the arms of God, and God will see us through, but we have to have the faith of a grain of mustard seed that God can and that God will. Do I have any believers in the room today?

God kept Abraham in suspense right up to the very end, and God will keep us in suspense but we have to wait upon the Lord and be of good courage, and he shall strengthen our hearts. Wait I say, wait I say, wait I say on the Lord.

The last thing I want to bring to your attention in this message is I want to ask you a question: Do you have what it takes to stand? Genesis 22:7-8 reads, "But Isaac spoke to Abraham his father and said, 'My father!' And he said, 'Here I am, my son.' Then he said, 'Look, the fire and the wood, but where is the lamb for a burnt offering?' And Abraham said, 'My son, God will provide for Himself the lamb for a burnt offering.' So the two of them went together." Not one time did Abraham tell Isaac, "My son, you are the sacrifice," but the text says that Abraham told Isaac that "God will provide for Himself the lamb."

Now, God had given Abraham a promise back in chapter 12 that he would make him a great nation, and that in him all the families of the earth would be blessed. Here is Abraham with his only seed who could possibly bring about that blessing, so Abraham had to go the rounds with God like Mohammed Ali went the rounds with George Foreman.

In round one God throws a right punch to Abraham's chest where his heart is by telling Abraham to kill his only son, but the punch doesn't knock Abraham out. Abraham staggers but stays in the ring with God. In round two God throws a punch to Abraham's head by telling him to offer Isaac as a burnt sacrifice. Abraham grabs his head because he can't believe what God is saying, but Abraham is still standing. In round three God throws Abraham a punch in his stomach by allowing Abraham to lay Isaac upon the altar, upon the wood. From that punch Abraham bends but he doesn't break. In the fourth round God throws Abraham a punch to the ribs when He allows Abraham to stretch out the knife to slay his son, and although Abraham has been hit in the chest, punched in the head, punched in his stomach, and knocked in his ribs, Abraham is still standing. Then from the balcony of heaven the bell rings, and God tells Abraham he is the heavyweight champion of the faith. Abraham had the promise from God, and Abraham stood on the promise.

Brothers and sisters in Christ, we too have the promise, and no matter what the test may be, we can stand on the promises of God. We have the promise that with God all things are possible. So no matter what, if it is impossible with man, it is possible for God, so stand on the promise.

We have the promise that if we seek first the kingdom of God and his righteousness, then all these things shall be added unto us. What things, Bishop? The things are food, finance, and fashion, so stand on the promise. We have the promise that if we ask, it will be given; if we seek, we shall find; and if we knock, the door shall be opened unto us. So stand on that promise. We have the promise that if we follow God, we shall be the head and not the tail. We shall be above and not beneath; we shall be the lender and not the borrower. So stand on that promise. We have the promise that if we give, it shall be given unto us, good measure pressed down and running over. So stand on the promise. We have the promise that if we abide in him and his words abide in us, we shall ask whatever we will and it will be done unto us. So stand on the promise. We have the promise that we can do all things through Christ who strengthens us. So stand on the promise. We have the promise that if we forgive, we shall be forgiven. So stand on the promise. We have the promise that in everything we are more than conquerors through him who loved us. So stand on the promise. We have the promise that in due season we shall reap if we faint not. So stand on the promise. Then we have the promise that, if we hold on and if we hold out, when this life is over we shall receive a crown of righteousness. So stand on the promise.

All we need to stand is the promises of God. So I ask you today: Do you have his promise? Are you trusting in the promise? Are you standing on the promise? After you've done all you can do, just stand on the promise.

BIBLIOGRAPHY

Akin, Daniel L. *A Theology for the Church*. Nashville, TN: B&H Publishing Group, 2007.

Barth, Karl. *Prayer*. Louisville, KY: Westminster John Knox Press, 2002.

Barton, John. "Disclosing Human Possibilities: Revelation and Biblical Stories." In *Revelation and Story: Narrative Theology and the Centrality of Story*, edited by Gerhard Sauter and John Barton, 53–60. Burlington, VT: Ashgate Publishing, 2000.

Bausch, William J. *Storytelling: Imagination and Faith*. Mystic, CT: Twenty-Third Publications, 1989.

Beck, John A. *God as Storyteller: Seeking Meaning in Biblical Narrative*. St. Louis, MO: Chalice Press, 2008.

Bilezikian, Gilbert. *Community 101: Reclaiming the Church as a Community of Oneness*. Grand Rapids, MI: Zondervan Publishing House, 1997.

Bloesch, Donald G. *The Struggle of Prayer*. Colorado Springs, CO: Helmers & Howard Publishers, 1988.

Bonhoeffer, Dietrich. *Life Together: A Discussion of Christian Fellowship*. New York: Harper & Row Publishers, 1954.

Bounds, E. M. *The Weapon of Prayer*. New Kensington, PA: Whitaker House, 1996.

Borg, Marcus J. *Reading the Bible Again for the First Time: Taking the Bible Seriously but Not Literally.* San Francisco, CA: HarperSanFrancisco, 2001.

Brockelman, Paul. *The Inside Story: A Narrative Approach to Religious Understanding and Truth.* New York: State University of New York Press, 1992.

Elwell, Walter A. *Evangelical Dictionary of Theology.* Grand Rapids, MI: Baker Academic, 1984.

Erickson, Millard J. *Christian Theology.* Grand Rapids, MI: Baker Book House, 1985.

Evans, James H., Jr. *We Have Been Believers.* Minneapolis, MN: Augsburg Fortress Publishers, 1992.

Foster, Richard. *Prayer: Finding the Heart's True Home.* San Francisco, CA: Harper Collins, 1992.

Frei, Hans W. *Theology and Narrative: Selected Essays.* New York: Oxford University Press, 1993.

Goldberg, Michael. *Theology and Narrative: A Critical Introduction.* Eugene, OR: Wipf and Stock Publishers, 1991.

Hauerwas, Stanley, and L. Gregory Jones, eds. *Why Narrative?: Readings in Narrative Theology.* Eugene, OR: Wipf and Stock Publishers, 1997.

Holt, Bradley P. *Thirsty for God: A Brief History of Christian Spirituality.* Minneapolis, MN: Fortress Publishers, 2005.

Jeremiah, David. *Prayer, the Great Adventure.* Sisters, OR: Multnomah Publishers, 1997.

Kepnes, Steven. *The Text as Thou: Martin Buber's Dialogical Hermeneutics and Narrative Theology.* Bloomington, IN: Indiana University Press, 1992.

Killinger, John. *Prayer: The Act of Being with God.* Waco, TX: Word Books, 1981.

Kinlaw, Dennis. *Let's Start with Jesus: A New Way of Doing Theology.* Grand Rapids, MI: Zondervan Publishing, 2005.

Kraus, Norman C. *The Community of the Spirit: How the Church Is in the World.* Eugene, OR: Wipf and Stock Publishers, 1993.

Lloyd-Jones, Martyn. *Studies in the Sermon on the Mount,* 2 vols. Grand Rapids, MI: Eerdmans, 1979.

Lodahl, Michael. *The Story of God: Wesleyan Theology and Biblical Narrative.* Kansas City, MO: Beacon Hill Press, 1994.

Loughlin, Gerard. *Telling God's Story: Bible, Church and Narrative Theology.* New York: Cambridge University Press, 1996.

MacArthur, John. *Alone with God: Rediscovering the Power and Passion of Prayer.* Colorado Springs, CO: David C. Cook, 1992.

Massey, James Earl. *When Thou Prayest.* Anderson, IN: Warner Press, 1960.

Nouwen, Henri J. M. *Intimacy.* San Francisco, CA: HarperSanFrancisco, 1969.

———. *Reaching Out: Three Movements of Spiritual Life.* London: HarperCollins Publishers, 1997.

Patton, Jeffrey H. *If It Could Happen Here: Turning the Small-Membership Church Around.* Nashville, TN: Abingdon Press, 2002.

Pennington, M. Basil. *Centering Prayer: Renewing an Ancient Christian Prayer Form.* Garden City, NY: Doubleday, 1980.

Reinberger, Francis E. *How to Pray*. Philadelphia, PA: Fortress Press, 1964.

Ryle, J. C. *Luke*. The Crossway Classic Commentaries. Wheaton, IL: Crossway Books, 1997.

Sanders, J. Oswald. *Effective Prayer*. Chicago, IL: Moody, 1969.

Spurgeon, Charles H. *The Power of Prayer in a Believer's Life*. Lynwood, WA: Emerald Books, 1993.

Stafford, Gilbert W. *Theology for Disciples: Systematic Considerations about the Life of Christian Faith*. Anderson, IN: Warner Press, 1996.

Strong, James. *Strong's Expanded Exhaustive Concordance of the Bible*. Nashville, TN: Thomas Nelson Publishers, 2001.

Stroup, George W. *The Promise of Narrative Theology: Recovering the Gospel in the Church*. Atlanta, GA: John Knox Press, 1944.

Tilley, Terrence W. *Story Theology*. Theology and Life Series 12. Wilmington, DE: Michael Glazier, 1985.

Torrey, R. A. *What the Bible Teaches: The Truths of the Bible Made Plain, Simple and Understandable*. Peabody, MA: Hendrickson Publishers, 1998.

van Deusen Hunsinger, Deborah. *Pray without Ceasing: Revitalizing Pastoral Care*. Grand Rapids, MI: William B. Eerdmans Publishing, 2006.

Wagner, C. Peter. *Churches That Pray*. Ventura, CA: Regal Publishers, 1993.

Willard, Dallas. *Hearing God: Developing a Conversational Relationship with God*. Downers Grove, IL: InterVarsity Press, 1999.